Follow the Dots... to Dazzling Quilts

JOAN SEGNA and JAYME CROW

Martingale®
& COMPANY

Dedication

This book is dedicated to my father, Dave Berglin.

Thank you for always supporting my artistic efforts. When I was a young girl, you admired and encouraged my efforts and shared with me your "fancy doodles." When I was a young mother entering the artistic world, you faithfully purchased my creations, stating, "Mom and I need this."

When I started quilting, I made you your very own quilt, and the inscription on the back says it all: "Stars for your patriotism and plaids for the shirts I remember you wearing when I was a little girl. Stitched into a quilt to keep you warm." Now you proudly tell your friends that "Jayme makes blankets—she made one for me!"

And to my mother, Bernie Berglin.

You are the one who encouraged me to learn to sew. And you were always tolerant of my "creative messes."

Thank you for encouraging two of my greatest joys—sewing and quilting. You still use my first cobbled-together flannel quilt to cuddle the grandchildren while you read to them.

—Jayme

Follow the Dots . . . to Dazzling Quilts
© 2005 by Joan Segna and Jayme Crow

That Patchwork Place® is an imprint of
Martingale & Company®.

Martingale & Company
20205 144th Avenue NE
Woodinville, WA 98072-8478 USA
www.martingale-pub.com

Credits

President .... Nancy J. Martin
CEO .... Daniel J. Martin
VP and General Manager .... Tom Wierzbicki
Publisher .... Jane Hamada
Editorial Director.................... Mary V. Green
Managing Editor .... Tina Cook
Technical Editor .... Ellen Pahl
Copy Editor............................ Durby Peterson
Design Director....................... Stan Green
Illustrator .... Robin Strobel
Cover and Text Designer .... Stan Green
Photographer .... Brent Kane

Printed in China
10 09 08 07 06 05   8 7 6 5 4 3 2 1

Library of Congress Cataloging-in-Publication Data
Segna, Joan.
    Follow the dots . . . to dazzling quilts / Joan Segna and Jayme Crow.
        p. cm.
    ISBN 1-56477-597-6
    1. Patchwork—Patterns. 2. Quilting. 3. Dots (Art)
I. Crow, Jayme. II. Title.
    TT835.S443 2005
    746.46'041—dc22
                                                    2005003480

Mission Statement • Dedicated to providing quality products and service to inspire creativity.

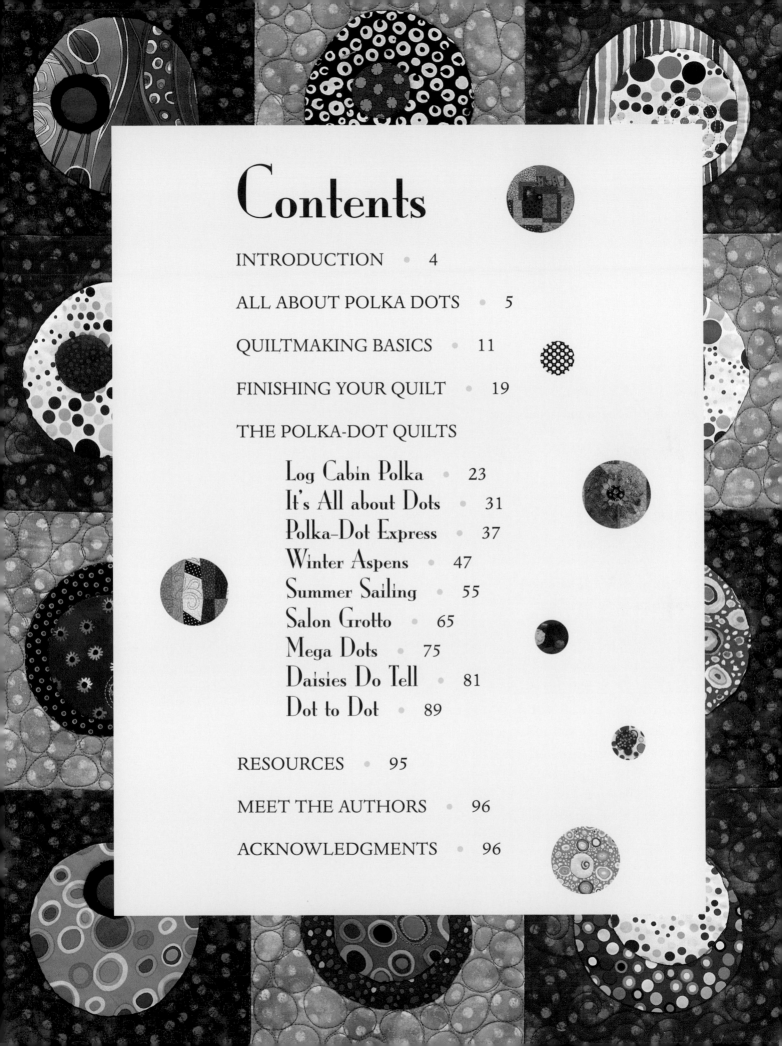

Contents

Introduction

Polka-dot fabrics have been around for as long as most of us can remember, probably since fabric was created! From our childhoods, we remember dotted Swiss for sweet frilly dresses, polka-dotted clown costumes, large polka dots in the early seventies, bold dots for contemporary pillows and all the myriad of dots in between. To those who love polka dots as we do—this book is for you!

We have long had a love affair with polka dots. In the explosion of new fabrics for the quilting industry, fabric designers often add a polka dot to a fabric line. Multiply that polka-dot fabric by three or four colorways, and voilá! Polka dots now reign in their own right.

Of course, we use a broad definition for the polka dot. Any shape resembling a circle is admitted into the not-so-exclusive polka-dot family. Even fabrics with just a few dots here and there are admitted for membership. As the designer of your own quilt, you are free to choose who's in and who's out of your polka-dot world.

After experiencing this book, you will see polka dots in a whole new light. You, too, may become a polka-dot addict, and for that, we are sorry. There is no cure. The only way to keep this condition under control is to use the dot fabrics in your quilts—adding a most delightful quality. This, in turn, gives you the exclusive right to purchase more polka-dot fabric!

This book offers you, as a quilter, the chance to develop your skills at quiltmaking using a defined parameter of design—polka dots only. You will work with polka dots in a wide variety of colors, sizes, and shapes. By nar-rowing your focus to one fabric type, dotted fabrics, you are not overwhelmed with endless options.

Along the way, you'll be introduced to the "art quilt" form in a simple yet exciting way. When you challenge yourself to create within a defined parameter, you grow as a designer and an artist. Often, it forces you to be creative to fill a void. For example, in case you don't have just the right polka-dot fabric, we share with you some ways to create your own polka dots.

So let's explore the many things we can do with polka-dot fabric. Imagine going on a "polka-dot-fabric hunt," looking for and seeing polka dots anew, expanding your definition of the polka dot, and envisioning exciting possibilities. Imagine getting together with your quilting friends for a "Polka-Dot Quilt Challenge." (Don't forget the M&Ms—the ultimate chocolate polka dots!)

Polka dots are playful, and they appeal to the child within us. They release inhibitions and give us permission to "color outside the lines" and develop ideas that don't follow conventional rules. We no longer subscribe to the old rule that says "You can't wear pink and orange together!" We put pink, orange, and purple together with unabashed abandon. The results can be stunning, whimsical, or contemporary. So, to all our quilting friends, we say, "Polka with dots!" It's a delightful exercise!

—Joan and Jayme

All about Polka Dots

In order to keep track of the whole family of polka dots, we came up with a system to identify our dots. Our reasoning is this: If they are categorized and have an "official" name, then they belong on the polka-dot family tree. Each category plays a distinctive role in design, which we discuss below. And now, without further ado, we introduce the stars of the show—the polka dots and their cousins.

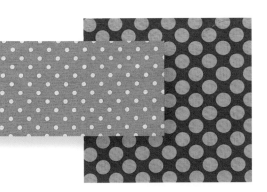

Traditional Polka Dots

These are the old-fashioned, classic, round polka dots. It's basic polka-dot fabric with symmetrical, evenly spaced dots and definite distinction between the dot color and the background color. These dots march stiffly in straight rows up and down the fabric in perfect precision. Like the chorus line, they add punch and definition to your quilts.

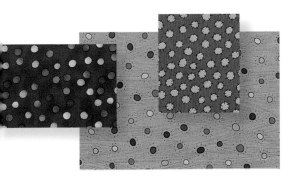

Random Dots

These are dots randomly placed on the background, and they can be in a wide variety of colors. Random dots are more playful than polka dots; they are out of sequence, out of line, and not always the same size. Random dots can add a more organic feel.

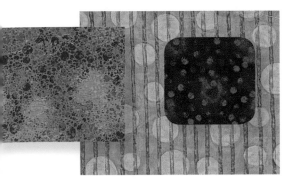

Muted Dots

These are subtle; they blend with the background either because they are a similar color or they are very small (minidots). At a distance, muted dots look like a solid fabric. Upon closer inspection, one discovers that the dots are indeed there, adding depth and interest. These are perfect as filler fabrics and backgrounds.

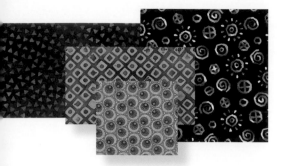

Almost Dots

These are unconventional dots! They are the unround dots, the square dots, and other funny-shaped dots. From a distance, they read as dots, so they are included as shirttail cousins in the big dot family.

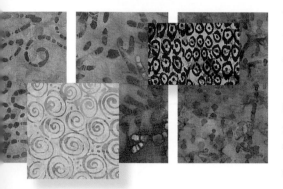

Not-Quite Dots

These are the most distant relatives of the polka-dot clan, and they are the rebels in the family. They are actually swirls, round squiggles, and other "interesting" dots. They add spice to the dot family, and when they show up, nothing is ever quite the same. They dance the polka with all the rest and add a playful and energizing force to the group.

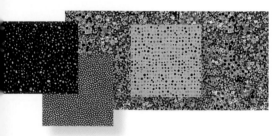

Speckled Dots

These are the smallest of the dot family; you could say they hail from Lilliput. They are perfect for backgrounds and for adding texture where needed.

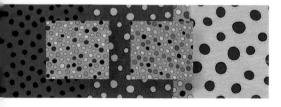

Clown Dots

Clown dots are the life of the party—big, bold, and sassy. When they show up, nothing is ever tame! These dots make a statement; there are no wallflowers here.

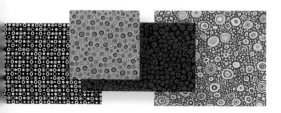

Donut Dots

These dots are unique because they have one or more dots within a dot. We call them "Donut Dots" because they remind us of those traditionally round and ever-popular treats with the hole in the middle. They're the airheads of the family!

Bubble Dots

Here we have the social butterflies of the polka-dot family, flitting here and there like bubbles on a breeze. You'll see these sprightly dots fit right in anywhere, from backgrounds to front-and-center stage.

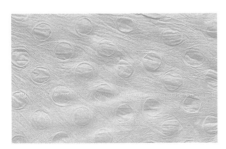

Retro Dots

Granny does the polka! These dots are a blast from the past, reminiscent of the thirties as well as the seventies. They meld the generations of dots together.

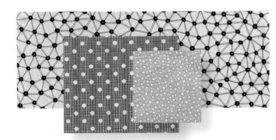

Not Just Dots

"Not Just Dots" are those that married outside their social circle; they have another shape printed along with them. These dots are very helpful in keeping the family reunions lively and interesting.

Textured Dots

These are the shyest dots and the subtlest of all. You have to look hard to see them, as they are dots of dimension and texture, not color.

Salon Grotto

Note the use of sharper, brighter dots in the foreground figures and muted dots in the background.

Log Cabin Polka

Fabrics in each quarter of the block are coordinated. They work nicely together around the common center.

Designing with Dots

Using dotted fabrics exclusively to create your entire design is an interesting challenge. You will want to choose dots from all the categories to define your design and allow one fabric to stand apart from another. Depending upon the project, you will need to carefully select your fabrics not only by color but also by dot size, dot intensity, dot placement, and dot density.

This may sound confusing and a bit baffling, but it is really quite simple once you get in tune with the dot family. For example, if you were creating "Salon Grotto," you would choose a flesh-colored small, muted dot that would read at a short distance as a solid flesh-tone fabric. It just wouldn't do to have a polka-dotted face looking like chicken pox! However, you can add small red dots to highlight round, rosy cheeks and elbows, and small black dots to "dot in" eyelashes. Conversely, dress fabrics can be a real polka dot, not a large, overwhelming dot, but a polka dot proportionate in size to the person's body. Various muted dots can create the backgrounds. Playing with dot color, dot size, and dot spacing can create an interesting look for the sofa and pillows. Remember that the foreground is in sharper focus and should consist of brighter colors; backgrounds are more muted shapes and colors.

Let's consider another example of designing with dots—"Log Cabin Polka." In this design, the strategy is to first determine the center-square fabric for each section of the block (each block is made up of four sections). Then, as you design each section, choose colors that enhance the center fabric and coordinate with each other. If each section of the block is pleasing, then when the four sections are put together they will work with each other. This quilt is so busy with dots and intense colors popping everywhere that your eye needs a place to rest, so we made the 2" center squares all the same color. This helps to identify each block and unify the quilt.

When arranging the blocks on a design wall, look for definite color breaks between the blocks to define them. This gives the quilt excitement and keeps your eye traveling over the quilt to discover all the fun you've designed into it.

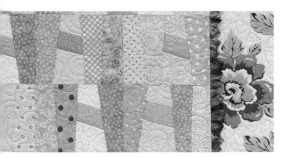

Polka-Dot Express

Silk petals surprise in the 3-D inner border. The large-scale floral border complements the polka dots and brings it all together charmingly.

Winter Aspens

Contrast is the name of the game. Juxtapose light against dark to create dimension, and layer small dots over large to add depth.

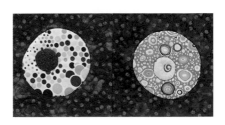

Mega Dots

Dots that aren't perfectly round and centered add interest and a whimsical, artistic quality to this quilt.

As you look through the photos of the quilts in the book, you will notice that we did not use dotted fabrics exclusively. Sometimes it's necessary to add a large floral as in "Polka-Dot Express" or a coordinating fabric as we did in the border of "Winter Aspens" to give the needed drama to a quilt. Experiment with other prints and solids to get the effect you wish.

Creative Dots

Sometimes we can't find a dot in just the right size, color, or design to suit our needs. Here is where your creative juices can really flow! Find the perfect color of fabric for your project and add your own dots by using beads, buttons, or fabric paint. In "Polka-Dot Express," we used a polka-dot stencil and fuchsia fabric paint to create the light pink fabric with fuchsia dots—just the right touch to complete our menu of fabrics.

Jayme hand-painted fuchsia dots onto light pink fabric for "Polka-Dot Express."

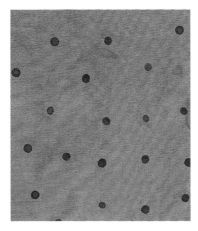

These dots were made on plain fabric with fabric paint and the handle tip of a paintbrush.

Another way to get just the right dots is to use appliqué. Choose the fabric that will work best, cut a circle, and appliqué it on, thus creating your own dots. We did this in "Mega Dots" and added another dimension to the dot theme.

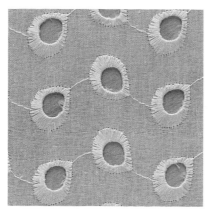

Salon Grotto

Finely stippled dots, made with a fabric pen, form cheeks and eyelashes.

Layer white eyelet with a colored background fabric to create dots.

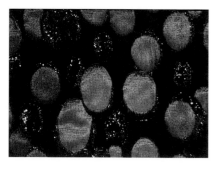

A lovely, sheer fabric with velvet dots was surprisingly easy to work with. We spray-glued it to cotton to use it as border fabric.

In "Salon Grotto," pink cheeks, lips, elbows, and hands were added with tiny dots from a fine-point permanent pen. Eyelashes were also dotted on.

More Ways to Dot Your Own Fabrics

When using fabric paints or dyes, the only limit is your imagination. For best results, choose PFD (prepared for dyeing) fabrics. These are white fabrics without any sizings, and they are available by the yard through several mail-order sources. See "Resources" on page 95 for more information.

Sun-reactive fabric paints: These paints are light sensitive. With them you can obtain shadow effects from objects placed on top of the wet fabric. Cut your fabric into small pieces, such as fat eighths or fat quarters. Tape the fabrics to a waterproof board along all four edges. Paint your fabric with sun-reactive fabric paint in the desired color, and place round objects on the fabric. Use metal washers, pennies, nickels, dimes, quarters, Cheerios, peanuts, anything you have around the house to create the look you want. Then place your fabric in the sun, with the round objects on top of the wet fabric, and wait for the prescribed amount of time. When the fabric is dry, you will have lighter polka dots where you placed the round objects—a unique piece of dotted cloth to add to your projects!

Embroidered-eyelet fabric: In "Polka-Dot Express," we used an embroidered eyelet backed by a color to create another dotted fabric. The eyelet, with its holes and satin stitch, adds a little dimension as well.

Dotted sheer fabrics: In "Mega Dots," we found a gorgeous sheer fabric in the evening-wear section and built the elegant version of our quilt around that fabric. We used a spray fabric adhesive to secure it to a cotton fabric and it quilted up beautifully. Of course, you will want to consider how the quilt will be cared for before adding fabrics that are more delicate or require dry cleaning.

Be on the lookout for unique ways to incorporate different fabrics into your overall design. Step out of the cotton box and see what you can find!

Quiltmaking Basics

Once you've met the polka-dot family and have your fabric, it's time to have some fun and make the quilts. Read on to learn all the basic techniques you'll need to make the quilts in this book.

Cutting

The instructions for rotary cutting are given for each project. All measurements include standard ¼" seam allowances.

1. Fold the fabric selvage to selvage, aligning the crosswise and lengthwise grains as much as possible. Place the folded edge of the fabric closest to you on the cutting mat. Align a square ruler, such as a Bias Square, along the folded edge of the fabric. Place a 6" x 24" ruler to the left of the square ruler, just covering the uneven raw edges of the left side of the fabric.

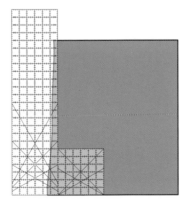

2. Remove the square ruler and cut along the right edge of the long ruler. Place your left hand firmly on the ruler and cut through both layers of fabric, along the right edge of the ruler; roll the rotary cutter away from you. Discard the strip. (Reverse this procedure if you are left-handed.)

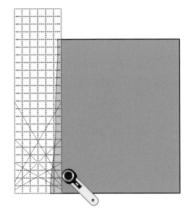

3. To cut strips, place the ruler over the fabric so that the newly cut edge of the fabric is aligned with the ruler markings at the required width. For example, if you need a 2" strip, the 2" line on the ruler should be directly over the straight edge of the fabric. Cut along the right edge of the ruler, again holding the ruler steady with your left hand. Cut halfway and then stop, leaving the rotary cutter in place. Move your left

hand up to hold the ruler securely along the length of the fabric and then finish the cut.

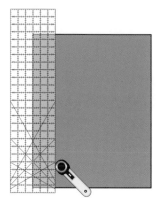

4. To cut squares or rectangles, cut strips first in the required widths. Trim the selvage ends off and rotate the strip so the cut ends are on the left. Align the ruler over the left edge of the strips at the correct ruler markings. Cut the strips into squares or rectangles as needed.

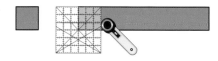

Machine Piecing

Maintaining a consistent ¼" seam allowance when piecing is the key to a successful quilt. Take time to establish an accurate ¼" seam guide on your machine. Some machines have a special presser foot that measures exactly ¼" from the center needle position to the edge of the foot. This feature allows you to use the edge of the foot to guide the fabric for a perfect ¼"-wide seam allowance.

If you don't have a ¼" presser foot, create a seam guide by placing the edge of a piece of tape, moleskin, or a magnetic seam guide ¼" away from the needle.

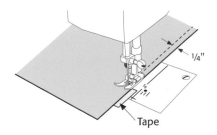

Pressing

Always press the seams of your pieces after sewing. Typically, seams are pressed to one side, toward the darker color whenever possible. First press the seams as they are sewn from the wrong side of the fabric to set the stitches. Then press them in the desired direction from the right side. Press carefully to avoid stretching or distortion.

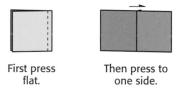

First press flat.   Then press to one side.

When sewing blocks into rows, plan ahead to press seam allowances in opposite directions from row to row. This reduces bulk and allows the seam allowances to butt together, making it easier to sew the rows together with perfectly matched seam intersections.

Opposing seams

Hand Appliqué

For simple appliquéd shapes such as circles and dots, we often use hand appliqué. We like the chance to relax with hand sewing, and it makes the project portable when traveling or waiting for appointments. To obtain crisp edges and smooth curves, use the following freezer-paper method.

1. Trace the pattern pieces for the quilt onto the dull side of the freezer paper to make your template. You will need one freezer-paper template for each shape. The templates do not include seam allowances.

2. Iron the freezer-paper template, shiny side down, onto the wrong side of the appliqué fabric. Cut out the shape, adding ¼" all around for seam allowances.

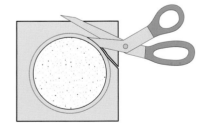

3. With a dry, hot iron, press the seam allowance over the freezer paper.

4. Pin the shape in place on the background.

PIN POINTER
Place pins on the wrong side of the fabric, and your thread won't get caught on them while stitching.

5. Thread an appliqué needle or Sharp (a standard hand-sewing needle) with an 18" length of thread in a color that matches the appliqué. Knot the thread tail.

6. Hide the knot by slipping the needle into the seam allowance from the wrong side of the appliqué piece, bringing it out on the fold line.

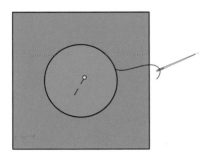

Hide knot in fold.

7. Work from right to left if you are right-handed and from left to right if you are left-handed. Insert the needle into the background right next to where the needle

came out of the folded edge of the appliqué shape. Bring the needle up through the edge of the appliqué, about ⅛" away from the first stitch. Catch just one or two threads of the appliqué.

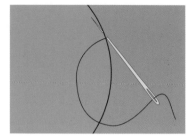

8. Pull the thread taut and take a second stitch into the background, right next to where the thread came up through the appliqué. Bring the needle up ⅛" away, catching the folded edge of the appliqué. Continue stitching in this manner.

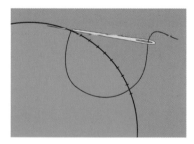

9. Stitch until there is a 1" opening. Gently remove the freezer paper and finish stitching around the shape. Another option is to stitch around the entire unit, and then make a 1" slit in the back and pull the paper out through the slit.

10. End your stitching on the wrong side of the fabric. Take a small stitch behind the appliqué piece and then insert the needle through the thread loop, before tightening, to make a knot. Repeat to make a second knot.

Machine Appliqué

For the landscapes and backgrounds of the pictorial quilts in this book, we use a machine-appliqué technique. With this method, you sew through all three layers of the quilt at once: the top, batting, and backing. You will use invisible nylon thread in your machine and sew with a blind hem stitch. This results in stitching that is hardly noticeable, and you are quilting at the same time.

You will need an open-toe embroidery foot to give yourself a clear view of the stitching. Use a size 60/8 fine machine needle because it will not leave big holes. For thread, we like YLI nylon invisible thread. It comes in clear for light fabrics and a smoke color for dark fabrics.

1. Thread the machine with the nylon thread on top and a thread that matches the backing fabric in the bobbin. Select the blind hem stitch, setting it to make three to seven straight stitches to one zigzag.

2. Prepare the appliqué shapes using the patterns or cutting instructions provided with each quilt. You will need a ¼" seam allowance around each shape. Fold the seam allowance under and press to the wrong side.

3. Pin the shape in place on the background and stitch along the edge, just next to the appliqué. The zigzag stitch will take a "bite" into the appliqué to hold it in place.

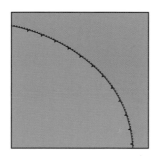

4. Practice sewing on scrap fabrics to adjust the length and width of the zigzag stitch so that it just catches the fold of the fabric. To end the stitching around a shape, overlap your starting stitches by about ½".

Fusible Appliqué

This fast and fun method of appliqué uses fusible web to adhere appliqué shapes to the background fabric. We've used this technique for appliqué shapes that have a lot of detail or for smaller shapes that are more difficult to sew with the blind hem stitch. The smaller details of the pictorial quilts on pages 55 and 65 are fused, as are the flowers in "Daisies Do Tell" on page 81. If the appliqué designs are asymmetrical or directional, the patterns are drawn onto the fusible web in reverse.

READ THE DIRECTIONS
Be sure to read the manufacturer's directions for the specific brand of fusible web that you are using. The directions can vary slightly from one brand to the next.

1. Trace the shape onto the paper side of the fusible web. Roughly cut out the shape, leaving a ½" margin all around the drawn line.

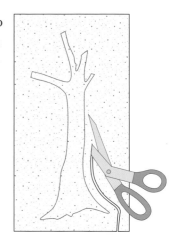

2. Fuse the shapes to the wrong side of the chosen fabric with your iron set at the temperature recommended by the manufacturer.

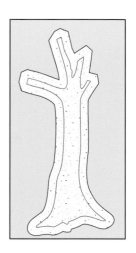

3. Cut out the shape on the drawn line. (The small inner flowers of "Daisies Do Tell" are an exception to this procedure. Follow the step-by-step instructions for that quilt.)

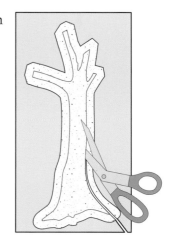

4. Remove the paper backing and position the shape on the background. Fuse it in place with your iron.

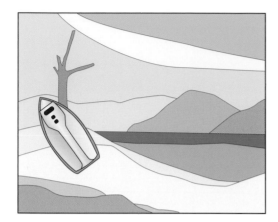

5. Some projects direct you to stitch the edges of the appliqués with a blanket stitch or zigzag stitch; others include quilting stitches that add details to the fused appliqués.

Adding Borders

The cutting list for each project will indicate the width and number of strips to cut from the border fabric(s). Cut the strips across the fabric width, from selvage to selvage. The strips will be trimmed to the required length or pieced to make strips long enough to border the quilt.

To add borders to your quilt, follow these steps:

1. Measure the quilt through the center from top to bottom. Cut two border strips to this measurement. If the length is longer than 42", sew two strips together. We often sew border strips using a diagonal seam (refer to step 1 of "Binding" on page 20), but you can sew them with a straight seam if desired. Trim the strip to the measured length. Mark the centers of both sides of the quilt and the centers of the border strips. Match the centers and the ends, and stitch the strips to the sides of the quilt top. Press the seams toward the borders.

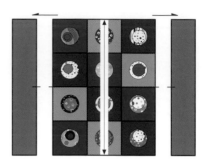

Measure center of
quilt, top to bottom.
Mark centers.

2. Measure the width of the quilt from side to side, including the border strips just added. Cut two border strips to this measurement, piecing as necessary. Mark the center of the quilt top and bottom edges and the center of the border strips. Sew the strips to the top and bottom edges of the quilt top, matching centers and ends. Press the seams toward the borders.

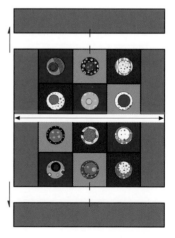

Measure center of quilt, side to
side, including border strips.
Mark centers.

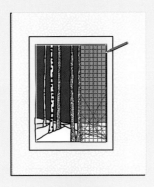

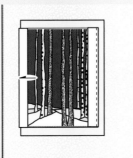

Stitch on chalk line.

SQUARING UP

The pictorial quilts in this book are sewn and quilted before borders are added. This allows you to do the appliqué and quilting at the same time. Quilting first also gives you the opportunity to "square up" the center of the quilt before adding border strips. The stitching can sometimes create sides that are not perfectly straight and corners that are not quite square.

Using your 6" x 24" rotary ruler, or a large square ruler, draw a chalk line along each edge of the quilt to mark a straight positioning line for the borders. Make sure the corners are square, but don't cut excess batting and backing in the squaring-up process. Square up only by marking with chalk.

Pin the border strips on, using the chalk line as a guide. Sew the border strips on through all layers. Trim the seams to ¼" if needed.

Embellishments

Embellishing a project adds that little twist to make the project unique. Embellishments can also direct the eye and become a part of the design element or add a little color punch to take your project out of the ordinary. If the project still just doesn't feel quite complete, or needs some extra touch, follow your instincts to judiciously add an unexpected color or textural embellishment detail. See "Resources" on page 95 to find some of the embellishments mentioned here.

Ribbons

Ribbons are always a wonderful embellishment. To accent your polka-dot fabrics, look for ribbons with dots. They add wonderful texture and spark to any project. Or, add your own dots to plain ribbons by painting or dyeing them. You can also stitch round buttons onto the ribbons to form a playful array of dimensional dots. Silk ribbons can be scrunched and manipulated to create a myriad of flowers, leaves, stems, or abstract designs.

Dotted ribbons

Buttons

We have a running joke at our studio—when in doubt reach for the buttons! We have jars full, and each button has its own personality. Some need to be clustered to make a statement, and some can make that statement all on their own. Never underestimate the power of a button! Try arranging them symmetrically, but also try arranging in a more random way. Pay attention to the color you choose—that is where the added punch comes in!

Other Embellishments

Never overlook other embellishments, such as lace, rickrack, yarns, braids, beads, paint, and dimensional petals. The added texture of dimensional embellishment allows the eye an unexpected place to rest and adds a unique design element. Unexpected touches in a quilt are what give it personality and distinction.

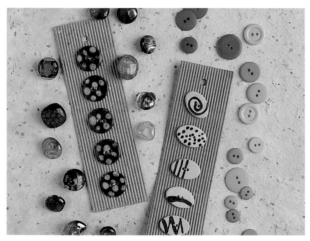

Buttons can be tactile polka dots.

Embellishments such as beads, ribbons, and dimensional petals add texture to a quilt.

Dimensional petals form an inner border.

Joan fused ribbons onto "Dot to Dot" and then attached dichroic glass buttons at the intersections.

Finishing Your Quilt

There's always a feeling of accomplishment when you've completed your quilt top, but it's not a finished quilt yet! This section provides the basics of the finishing techniques you'll need to complete your quilt and enjoy it for years to come.

Marking the Quilting Design

If you plan to use a quilting design that needs to be marked, now is the time to mark the quilt top, before you layer it with batting and backing. Test the marking tool on a scrap of the quilt fabric first to make sure the marks can be easily removed. If you are planning to quilt in the ditch (in the seam lines) or free-motion quilt randomly, there is no need to mark the design.

Layering and Basting

Give your quilt a final pressing and take the batting out of the package to let it relax before you assemble the quilt layers. Cut the backing and batting 3" to 4" larger than the quilt top on all sides. The batting and backing can draw up as the quilt is quilted. For quilts wider than 40", it will be necessary to piece two or three lengths of backing fabric together to make a piece the required size. If piecing is required, trim away the selvages before stitching. Piece the backing with either a horizontal or vertical seam to make the most efficient use of your fabric. Press the seams open to make quilting easier. You can also piece your backing from leftover fabrics and be as creative as you like.

To assemble the layers, lay the backing wrong side up on a flat surface, such as a tabletop or floor. Smooth out the wrinkles and secure the edges with masking tape or binder clips, making sure the fabric is taut but not stretched. Place the batting over the backing and smooth out any wrinkles, working from the center out. Center the pressed top over the batting right side up. Smooth out any wrinkles. If you are machine quilting, use rustproof safety pins to pin the layers together. Place the pins approximately 4" to 6" apart.

If you are hand quilting, thread baste the layers together in a grid of stitches. Begin at the center and work outward.

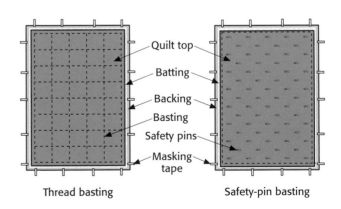

Quilt top
Batting
Backing
Basting
Safety pins
Masking tape

Thread basting   Safety-pin basting

Quilting

We've all heard the saying "Quilting makes the quilt." It certainly can enhance your design and add dimension, whether you are quilting by hand or machine. Circles, swirls, and spirals are good complementary designs for the polka-dot quilts. Look at the photographs for each project to get ideas, but remember that quilting designs are truly your choice.

No matter which quilting method you use, begin by stabilizing the layers. This can be done by quilting along the block edges or stitching in the ditch of each seam. Begin in the center of the quilt and work outward. If you are machine quilting, a walking foot is invaluable for feeding the layers evenly through the machine.

Binding

Consider the binding to be the outermost portion of the frame you create around your quilt. Audition fabrics for the binding just as you would for the borders.

The cutting instructions for each project give the number of 2¼"-wide strips to cut. Cut the strips across the width of the fabric. If you use a lofty batting, consider cutting your strips 2½" wide. You will need enough strips to go around the perimeter of the quilt plus 10" for corners and joining. The yardage requirements allow enough fabric for you to cut 2½" strips if needed.

1. Stitch the binding strips together with a diagonal seam to create one long strip. Cross the ends of two strips right sides together at right angles. Use a sharp pencil or fabric marker to draw a diagonal line across the strips as shown. Then stitch on the marked line. Trim the seam allowance to ¼" and press the seam open.

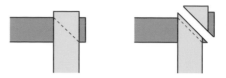

2. Trim one end of the binding strip at a 45° angle. Press under ¼" on the angled end. Press the binding strip in half, wrong sides together.

Fold line

3. Trim the backing and batting even with the quilt top, squaring up the corners as you trim.

4. Open the angled end of the binding and place the binding along the edge of the quilt top, several inches from a corner. Align the binding and quilt raw edges. Stitch through one binding thickness for about 3", using a ¼"-wide seam allowance; backstitch and cut the threads.

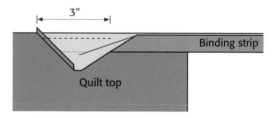

3"

Binding strip

Quilt top

> ## USE A WALKING FOOT
> A walking foot or an even-feed foot is helpful for attaching bindings. It feeds all the layers through the machine evenly.

5. Refold the binding so it is doubled. Continue stitching where you left off, through both binding thicknesses. End the stitching ¼" from the corner of the quilt and backstitch. Clip the threads.

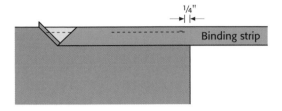

6. Turn the quilt so you will be ready to sew down the next side. Fold the binding strip up at a 45° angle and then back down on itself, aligning the raw edges with the edge of the quilt. Begin stitching ¼" from the corner and backstitch to secure the stitches. Continue sewing the binding to the quilt, ending the stitching ¼" from the corner; backstitch and clip the threads.

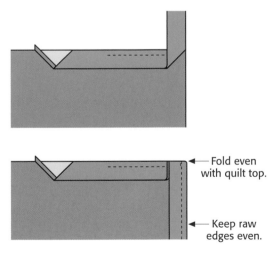

7. Repeat the same procedure for the remaining corners. When you reach the beginning of the binding strip, stop stitching and leave the needle in the binding. Trim the end of the binding so it is just long enough to tuck inside the pocket formed by the single thickness. Tuck the end of the binding into the pocket and continue stitching through all thicknesses; backstitch.

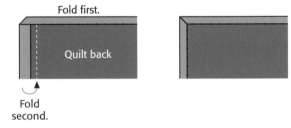

8. Fold the binding to the back of the quilt and hand stitch it in place. A miter will form at each corner. Blindstitch the mitered corners in place.

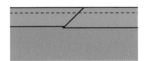

Log Cabin Polka

This scrappy derivative of a Log Cabin quilt hearkens back to the early days of our country. Scraps of fabric and usable pieces of clothing were recycled into warm bed quilts. Bright colors were especially treasured because they added a touch of sparkle and cheer. So, turn on the polka music, dig into your scrap bag, and create a one-of-a-kind treasure!

—Jayme

Pieced by Jayme Crow. Machine quilted by Sandy Sims.

Finished quilt: 56" x 74½"
Finished block: 18½" x 18½"
Number of blocks: 12

Materials

We like a very scrappy look, so we chose to use different fabrics in every block and purposely tried not to use the same polka-dot fabric twice. Refer to "Designing with Dots" on page 8 for a discussion of choosing fabrics for this quilt. See the second option on page 28 for a less scrappy version. That quilt uses just 14 different fabrics; each block, made up of four sections, is the same.

Yardage is based on 42"-wide fabric.

- 168 pieces of fabric, 10" x 13", for blocks*

- ⅛ yard of black print for block centers

- 3½ yards of fabric for backing

- ⅝ yard of fabric for binding

- 62" x 80" piece of batting

- Buttons for embellishing

See the cutting chart on page 24. You can use scraps for many of the pieces.

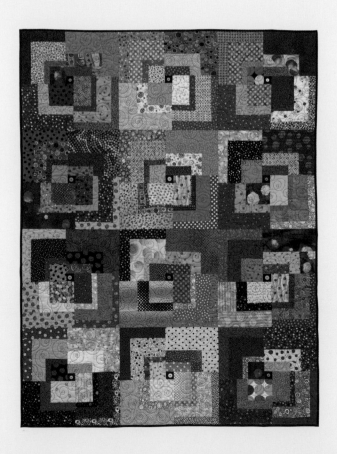

23

Cutting a Scrappy Quilt

To make a totally scrappy quilt, we recommend cutting just one block at a time. Use 14 different fabrics for each block and plan each block before cutting. Each 18½" square block is made up of four

units, referred to as units A, B, C, and D. Choose fabrics for each piece, and as you cut, label the pieces with the unit letter and the piece number. All measurements include ¼" seam allowances.

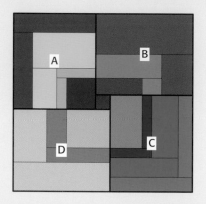
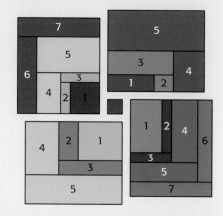

Fabric	Block Unit and Piece	Size to Cut
1	A-1	1 rectangle, 3½" x 3¾"
2	A-2	1 rectangle, 1½" x 3¾"
	A-3	1 rectangle, 1½" x 4½"
3	A-4	1 rectangle, 3" x 4¾"
	A-5	1 rectangle, 4¼" x 7"
4	A-6	1 rectangle, 2½" x 8½"
	A-7	1 rectangle, 2½" x 9"
5	B-1	1 rectangle, 2¼" x 5¼"
6	B-2	1 rectangle, 2¼" x 2½"
	B-3	1 rectangle, 3" x 7¼"
7	B-4	1 rectangle, 3¾" x 4¾"
	B-5	1 rectangle, 4¾" x 10½"
8	C-1	1 rectangle, 3¾" x 6"
9	C-2	1 rectangle, 1½" x 6"
	C-3	1 rectangle, 1½" x 4¾"
10	C-4	1 rectangle, 3¼" x 7"
	C-5	1 rectangle, 2½" x 7½"
11	C-6 and C-7	2 rectangles, 2" x 9"
12	D-1	1 rectangle, 4½" x 5"
13	D-2	1 rectangle, 2½" x 4½"
	D-3	1 rectangle, 2" x 7"
14	D-4	1 rectangle, 4" x 6"
	D-5	1 rectangle, 3½" x 10½"
Black print	Center square	1 square, 2" x 2"

Assembling the Blocks

Each segment of the block is pieced similar to a half Log Cabin block. The rectangles are sewn on to two alternating sides of the first piece in each unit. Refer to the illustrations and assemble the block units as directed below. Press after each seam is stitched, and press all seams away from the first piece in the unit.

1. Sew piece A-2 to the left edge of A-1.

2. Sew piece A-3 to the top edge of the unit just sewn.

3. Sew piece A-4 to the left edge of the unit.

4. Sew piece A-5 to the top edge of the unit.

5. Sew piece A-6 to the left edge of the unit.

6. Sew piece A-7 to the top edge of the unit. Press.

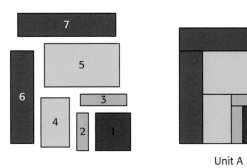

Unit A

7. Sew piece B-2 to the right edge of B-1.

8. Sew piece B-3 to the top edge of the unit just sewn.

9. Sew piece B-4 to the right edge of the assembled unit.

10. Sew piece B-5 to top edge of the unit.

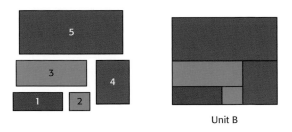

Unit B

11. Sew piece C-2 to the right edge of C-1.

12. Sew piece C-3 to the bottom edge of the unit just sewn.

13. Sew piece C-4 to the right edge of the unit.

14. Sew piece C-5 to the bottom edge of the unit.

15. Sew piece C-6 to the right edge of the unit.

16. Sew piece C-7 to the bottom edge of the unit.

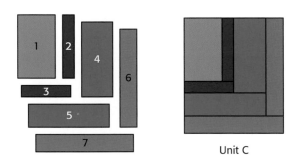

Unit C

17. Sew piece D-2 to the left edge of D-1.

18. Sew piece D-3 to the bottom edge of the unit just sewn.

19. Sew piece D-4 to the left edge of the unit.

20. Sew piece D-5 to the bottom edge of the unit.

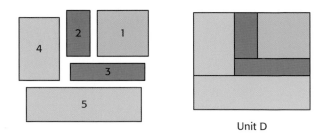

Unit D

21. To assemble the block units, you will sew around the 2" black-print center square counterclockwise, using a partial seam at the first join. With right sides together, line up the 2" square with the bottom of unit A as shown. Begin in the middle of the 2" square and stitch to the bottom edge of unit A. Press away from the center square.

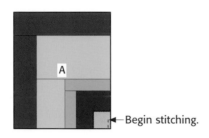

22. Sew unit D to the bottom edge of unit A and the 2" square. Press.

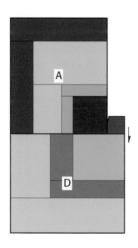

23. Sew unit C to the right edge of unit D and the 2" square. Press.

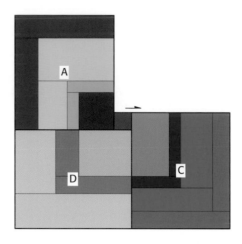

24. Before sewing unit B to the top edge of unit C and the 2" square, make sure the loose piece of unit A is out of the way. Sew unit B. Press away from the center square.

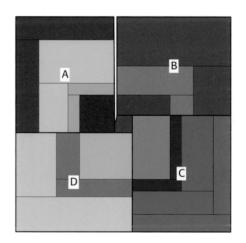

25. Sew the seam between unit A, the 2" square, and unit B, beginning in the middle of the 2" square. Press away from the center square. The block is complete. It should measure 19" x 19".

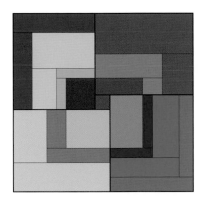

26. Repeat steps 1 through 25 to make the remaining 11 blocks.

Assembling the Quilt

1. Arrange the blocks in four rows of three blocks each.

2. Sew the blocks into rows. Press the seams in opposite directions from row to row.

3. Sew the rows together. Press the seams in one direction.

Finishing

Refer to "Finishing Your Quilt" on pages 19–21 for details as needed.

1. Prepare the backing by piecing it with a horizontal seam. Layer and baste the quilt with batting and backing.

2. Hand or machine quilt as desired.

3. Cut 7 strips 2¼" wide from the binding fabric. Make and attach the binding. Add buttons if desired.

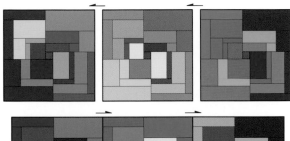

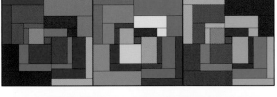

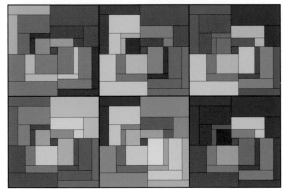

Log Cabin Polka II

For this version of "Log Cabin Polka," a total of 14 fabrics are used. The fabrics are repeated for each 18½" block; hence, each block will be the same. If you choose to make a quilt with just four blocks, the finished size will be 37½" x 37½".

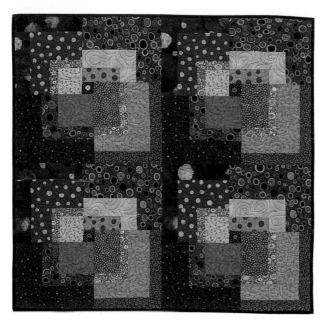

Pieced by Jayme Crow. Machine quilted by Sandy Sims.

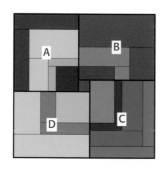

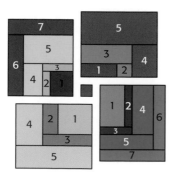

Materials

Yardage is based on 42"-wide fabric.

Block Unit and Piece	12-Block Quilt	4-Block Quilt
A-1	⅜ yard	¼ yard
A-2 / A-3	¼ yard	¼ yard
A-4 / A-5	⅝ yard	⅜ yard
A-6 / A-7	⅝ yard	¼ yard
B-1	¼ yard	⅛ yard
B-2 / B-3	½ yard	¼ yard
B-4 / B-5	⅞ yard	½ yard
C-1	⅜ yard	¼ yard
C-2 / C-3	¼ yard	¼ yard
C-4 / C-5	⅝ yard	¼ yard
C-6 / C-7	½ yard	¼ yard
D-1	⅜ yard	¼ yard
D-2 / D-3	½ yard	¼ yard
D-4 / D-5	¾ yard	½ yard
Block center	⅛ yard of black print	⅛ yard
Backing, Binding, Batting		
Backing	3½ yards	1¼ yards
Binding	⅝ yard	⅜ yard
Batting	62" x 80" piece	43" x 43" piece

Note: We've included the cutting for 12 blocks. To make a quilt with just 4 blocks, as shown in the photograph, use the column for the second cut in the chart on the opposite page, and cut 4 of each rectangle or square rather than 12.

Cutting for 12 Blocks

All measurements include ¼" seam allowances.

Fabric	Block Unit and Piece	Number and Size to Cut	Second Cut
1	A-1	2 strips, 3½" x 42"	12 rectangles, 3½" x 3¾"
2	A-2	3 strips, 1½" x 42"	12 rectangles, 1½" x 3¾"
	A-3		12 rectangles, 1½" x 4½"
3	A-4	2 strips, 3" x 42"	12 rectangles, 3" x 4¾"
	A-5	3 strips, 4¼" x 42"	12 rectangles, 4¼" x 7"
4	A-6	6 strips, 2½" x 42"	12 rectangles, 2½" x 8½"
	A-7		12 rectangles, 2½" x 9"
5	B-1	2 strips, 2¼" x 42"	12 rectangles 2¼" x 5¼"
6	B-2	1 strip, 2¼" x 42"	12 rectangles, 2¼" x 2½"
	B-3	3 strips, 3" x 42"	12 rectangles, 3" x 7¼"
7	B-4	2 strips, 3¾" x 42"	12 rectangles, 3¾" x 4¾"
	B-5	4 strips, 4¾" x 42"	12 rectangles, 4¾" x 10½"
8	C-1	2 strips, 3¾" x 42"	12 rectangles, 3¾" x 6"
9	C-2	4 strips, 1½" x 42"	12 rectangles, 1½" x 6"
	C-3		12 rectangles, 1½" x 4¾"
10	C-4	3 strips, 3¼" x 42"	12 rectangles, 3¼" x 7"
	C-5	3 strips, 2½" x 42"	12 rectangles, 2½" x 7½"
11	C-6	6 strips, 2" x 42"	12 rectangles, 2" x 9"
	C-7		12 rectangles, 2" x 9"
12	D-1	2 strips, 4½" x 42"	12 rectangles, 4½" x 5"
13	D-2	2 strips, 2½" x 42"	12 rectangles, 2½" x 4½"
	D-3	3 strips, 2" x 42"	12 rectangles, 2" x 7"
14	D-4	2 strips, 4" x 42"	12 rectangles, 4" x 6"
	D-5	4 strips, 3½" x 42"	12 rectangles, 3½" x 10½"
Black print	Center square	1 strip, 2" x 42"	12 squares, 2" x 2"

Backing and Binding	**12-Block Quilt**	**4-Block Quilt**
Backing	2 pieces, 63" x 42"	1 piece, 42" x 42"
Binding	7 strips, 2¼" x 42"	4 strips, 2¼" x 42"

Assembling the Blocks and Quilt

Follow the instructions beginning on page 25 for the scrappy version to make the 12 identical blocks. Sew the blocks together as directed in "Assembling the Quilt" on page 27. Finish the quilt as directed on page 27.

RETREAT TIP
Have 12 participants each bring the fabric needed (14 fabrics plus a black print) for the less scrappy version of the 12-block quilt. Swap one block's worth of strips with each person. Each quilter ends up with 168 fabrics for a scrappy quilt.

It's All about Dots

Use your favorite polka-dot fabrics, add fun embellishments, and this whimsical table runner is sure to please, whether it's for yourself or for a gift. One Christmas I received a funky switch plate: a rusty angel holding a heart. A curious gift, I thought at the time. But every time I reach for that light switch, it makes me smile. What a bonus! I hope this polka-dot table runner does the same for you.

—Joan

Pieced by Joan Segna. Quilted by Sandy Sims.

Finished table runner: 19½" x 59½"
Finished Snowball block: 4" x 4"

Materials

Yardage is based on 42"-wide fabric.

- 1⅛ yards of black polka-dot fabric for block borders, outer border, and binding

- ½ yard of khaki green polka-dot fabric for Snowball block corners and borders

- 10 fat eighths of coordinating colors for Snowball blocks

- 5 fat eighths of coordinating colors for center squares

- 4 squares, 9" x 9", of striped fabric for center dots

- 1⅞ yards of fabric for backing

- 27" x 67" piece of batting

- 2 sheets of lightweight fusible web, 9" x 12"

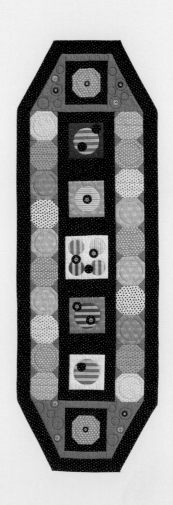

Cutting

All measurements include ¼" seam allowances.

From the khaki green polka-dot fabric, cut:

4 strips, 1½" x 42"; crosscut into 80 squares, 1½" x 1½"

2 strips, 1½" x 42"; crosscut into:
- 4 pieces, 1½" x 6½"
- 4 pieces, 1½" x 8½"

2 pieces, 4¾" x 9⅜"

From *each* of the 10 coordinating fat eighths, cut:

2 squares, 4½" x 4½"

From *each* of 2 of the fat eighths, cut:

1 square, 4½" x 4½"

From the black polka-dot fabric, cut:

8 strips, 2" x 42"; crosscut 4 into:
- 8 pieces, 2" x 5½"
- 8 pieces, 2" x 8½"
- 1 piece, 2" x 24" (for small dots)
- Reserve 4 strips for the borders

3 strips, 1½" x 42"; crosscut into:
- 8 squares, 1½" x 1½"
- 4 pieces, 1½" x 4½"
- 6 pieces, 1½" x 6½"
- 2 pieces, 1½" x 8½"

5 binding strips, 2¼" x 42"

From the 5 coordinating fat eighths, cut a total of:

4 squares, 5½" x 5½"

1 square*, 6½" x 6½"

This will be the center square in the table runner.

Constructing the Snowball Blocks

1. For the border Snowball blocks, draw a diagonal line from corner to corner on the wrong side of each 1½" khaki square.

2. Place a marked square on each of the four corners of a 4½" square. Stitch on the drawn lines. Trim ¼" beyond the stitching line and press the triangles toward the corners. Make 20 Snowball blocks. The blocks should measure 4½" x 4½".

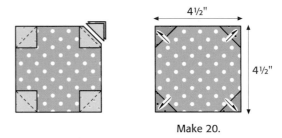

Make 20.

3. Draw a diagonal line from corner to corner on the wrong side of each 1½" black square.

4. For the end blocks, repeat step 2 to make two more Snowball blocks using the eight black squares and the two remaining 4½" squares.

5. Sash the two Snowball blocks made in step 4 by sewing one 1½" x 4½" black piece to the top and bottom of each block. Press toward the sashing. Sew a 1½" x 6½" black piece to each side of the two Snowball blocks. Press.

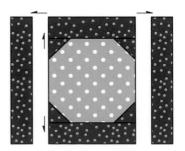

6. Sew a 1½" x 6½" khaki piece to the top and bottom of each Snowball block from step 5. Press. Sew a 1½" x 8½" khaki piece to each side of the two Snowball blocks. Press.

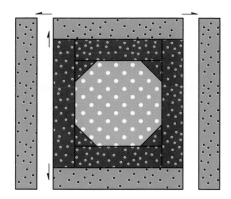

Constructing the Center Block

1. Sew one 2" x 5½" black piece to each side of a 5½" square cut from the coordinating fabrics. Sew a 2" x 8½" black piece to the top and bottom of the block. Repeat to make four blocks.

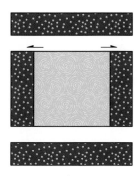

Make 4.

2. Sew a 1½" x 6½" black piece to the top and bottom of the 6½" square that will become the center block. Press. Sew a 1½" x 8½" black piece to the sides.

Make 1.

Assembling the Quilt

1. Lay out a row of 10 Snowball blocks, using one block of each color, on a design wall. Refer to the quilt diagram on page 34. When you are satisfied with the arrangement, number the blocks, if desired, and sew them together. Press all the seams in the same direction. Repeat to make a second row of 10 Snowball blocks, laying them out in the same order as the first row. Press the seams.

2. Sew the five center blocks together to form an 8½" x 40½" strip. Make sure that the larger block is in the middle. Press the seams in the opposite direction from the Snowball rows.

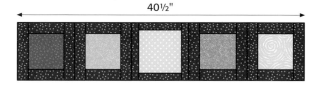

40½"

3. Use the circle patterns on page 35 to make templates. Trace four 3½" circles, four 2" circles, and nine 1¼" circles on the paper side of the fusible web. Cut each circle ½" beyond the pencil line. Refer to "Fusible Appliqué" on page 15.

4. Following the manufacturer's instructions, fuse one 3½" circle and one 2" circle to the wrong side of each of the four 9" striped squares. Cut out the circles on the drawn line.

5. Refer to the photo on page 30 and the quilt diagram on page 34. Remove the paper backing and center one 3½" circle on each of the four 5" x 5" blocks. Fuse in place.

6. Place the four 2" circles on the 6" middle square. Fuse in place.

7. Iron the nine 1¼" circles of fusible web to the wrong side of the 2" x 24" black piece. Cut out the circles on the drawn line. Arrange the circles on the center strip until you are pleased with the placement. You can use fewer circles if you prefer. Refer to the quilt photo on page 30. Fuse in place.

8. With right sides together, align the raw edges of one row of 10 Snowball blocks with the raw edges of the center row. Sew together and press the seams toward the center row. Reverse the order of Snowballs so that like colors aren't directly across each other on the table runner. Repeat to sew the second row of Snowball blocks to the other side of the center row. Press.

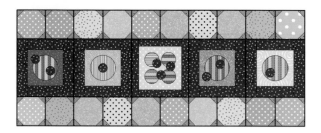

9. With a ruler and rotary cutter, cut the two 4¾" x 9⅜" khaki pieces in half diagonally.

Place rectangles right sides together, then cut on the diagonal.

10. Sew one khaki triangle to the right side of a bordered Snowball block. Sew a second khaki triangle to the left side of the block to make an end unit. Press. Make two.

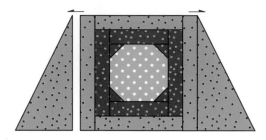

Make 2.

11. Match the seams of an end unit to each end of the assembled quilt top. Sew together and press the seams toward the end unit.

12. Center one 2" x 42" black border strip along one side of the quilt top, extending the strip about 1" at each end. Sew the strip to the side of the table runner. Press. Repeat on the other side.

13. Trim the ends even with the angled sides of the table runner as shown.

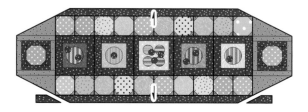

14. Cut the 2" black polka-dot strips to fit the four angled sides and sew them to the table runner. Trim the ends even with the sides

of the table runner. Then add the end borders to the table runner and trim.

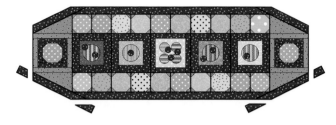

Finishing

Refer to "Finishing Your Quilt" on pages 19–21 for details as needed.

1. Layer and baste the table runner top with batting and backing.

2. Quilt in the ditch around the blocks, sashing, circles, and borders.

3. Make and attach the binding.

DOT FUN
Add flat buttons (with no shanks) here and there among your dots if desired.

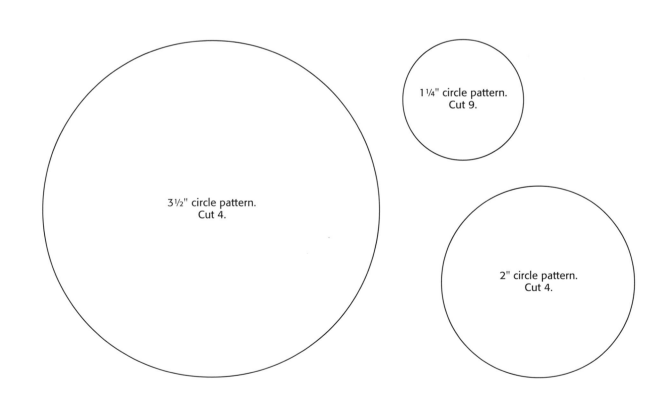

3½" circle pattern.
Cut 4.

1¼" circle pattern.
Cut 9.

2" circle pattern.
Cut 4.

Polka–Dot Express

These crazy-quilt-inspired blocks are filled with motion and fun. Each block includes polka-dot ribbon embellishment to create sparkle and diagonal movement. We added a romantic touch to the beribboned polka-dot blocks with a border of large-scale floral print and an inner border of Bella Nonna petals. (Thanks to our friend Debbie for naming this quilt!)

—Jayme

Pieced by Jayme Crow. Machine quilted by Sandy Sims.

Finished quilt: 37½" x 52½"
Finished block: 6½" x 8"

Materials

Yardage is based on 42"-wide fabric.

- 1⅛ yards of floral for outer border

- 2 fat quarters for blocks (piece A)

- 6 fat quarters for blocks (pieces B, C, and D)

- 1⅝ yards of fabric for backing

- ½ yard of fabric for binding

- 43" x 58" piece of batting

- 2¼ yards of 1½"-wide polka-dot ribbon

- 1 bag of Bella Nonna fuchsia petals for inner border (see "Resources" on page 95)

- 4½ yards of ¼"-wide fusible-web tape for attaching ribbon (optional)

Cutting

All measurements include ¼" seam allowances. See the fat quarter cutting guides below before you cut. You will have some extra pieces to give you choices when piecing. For the most efficient cutting, choose two of the fat quarters for the piece A portion of the blocks; that will be the background for the ribbons.

From *each* of the 2 fat quarters for piece A, cut:

5 strips, approximately 4" x 18"; crosscut each into 2 pieces, approximately 4" x 9" (20 pieces total)

From the polka-dot ribbon, cut:

18 pieces, 4" long

From *each* of the 6 fat quarters for pieces B, C, and D, cut:

5 strips, 3" x 18"; crosscut each into 2 pieces, 3" x 9" (60 pieces total)

From the floral outer-border fabric, cut:

5 strips, 7" x 42"

From the binding fabric, cut:

5 strips, 2¼" x 40"

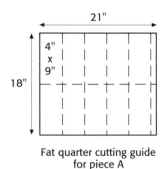

Fat quarter cutting guide
for piece A

Fat quarter cutting guide
for pieces B, C, and D

TIPS FOR PAPER PIECING

In paper piecing, a paper pattern copied or traced from the original is used as a foundation. It enables you to sew with accuracy without making templates for odd shapes. You sew fabric strips or pieces directly onto the paper, following the drawn stitching lines. Here are some helpful hints.

• When paper piecing, place fabrics against the unprinted side of the paper pattern, but stitch on the printed side, following the lines. To position fabric on the paper foundation, hold the pieces up to a light source or put the foundation on a light table.

• Sew with a smaller than normal stitch length (1.5) and use a large topstitching needle. This makes it easier to tear the paper away from the finished quilt block because you perforate the paper with the added stitches and a larger needle.

• Don't worry if you stitch a little off the seam line—this quilt is a crazy quilt and is very forgiving! Don't rip it out; just keep going.

• Make sure you have enough fabric for the outside seam allowance. It is easy to misjudge and come up short, so double check your piece before stitching. There is no need to backstitch your seams since you are sewing with a small stitch. Stitch a couple of stitches past the ends of the seam line.

• Square up your blocks before tearing off the paper backing.

Piecing the Blocks

1. Make 10 copies each of the block 1 and block 2 patterns on pages 45–46. You will use nine paper foundation patterns of each block for sewing; the tenth pattern is reserved for making a paper pattern for piece A.

2. Trim away excess paper from around each pattern, leaving ½" all around the solid line.

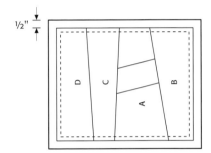

3. Using the extra paper pattern for block 1, cut out just piece A, adding ¼" all around. Repeat the process and make a paper pattern for the block 2 piece A; add a ¼" seam allowance all around.

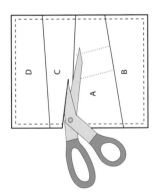

4. Use the block 1 piece A pattern to cut nine A pieces from the 4" x 9" fabric pieces. Place the paper pattern on the wrong side of the fabric and pin. Repeat for block 2 and cut nine A pieces from the remaining 4" x 9" fabric pieces.

5. Use a light table (or window) to help you place the ribbon pieces onto the right side of all A pieces. Place the paper pattern A behind the fabric A and place them on the light table. Pin a 4" piece of ribbon onto the right side of each A piece, using the diagonal lines as a guide. Stitch in place along the top and bottom edges of the ribbon or fuse the edges of the ribbon using the ¼" fusible-web tape.

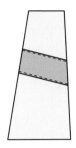

Stitch or fuse ribbon.

6. Pin a block 1 piece A with ribbon to each of the nine block 1 paper foundation patterns. Position each A piece right side up on the side of the paper foundation without lines. Each A piece should extend ¼" beyond the side lines and also beyond the top and bottom solid line. Place on a light table or hold up to the light to check.

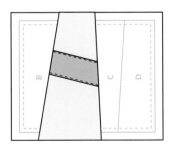

7. Place a piece B strip on piece A, with right sides together and edges aligned. Pin in place to secure.

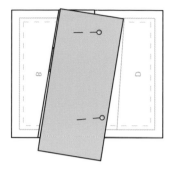

Place B fabric on top of piece A, right sides together.

8. Turn the block over and stitch with a short, straight stitch along the A/B seam line, securing piece A to piece B and the ribbon between.

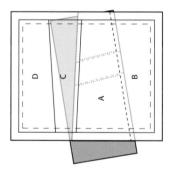

9. Turn the block back over and unpin the pieces. Turn to the right side of the paper; fold back the paper and crease on the line, exposing the excess fabric. Trim the excess

fabric, if necessary, to create a ¼" seam allowance. Press the seam between pieces A and B.

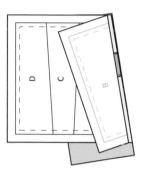

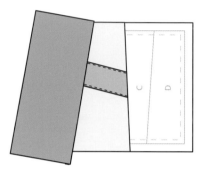

10. Place a piece C strip on piece A, with right sides together. Pin in place, aligning the edges.

11. Turn the block over and stitch the A/C seam. Turn the block back over and unpin the pieces. Fold back the paper and trim the seam allowance to ¼" if necessary. Press the seam between pieces A and C.

12. Place a piece D strip on piece C, with right sides together. Pin in place, aligning the edges.

13. Turn the block over and stitch the C/D seam. Turn the block back over and unpin the pieces. Fold back the paper and trim the seam allowance to ¼" if necessary. Press the seam between pieces C and D.

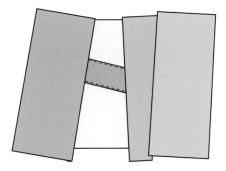

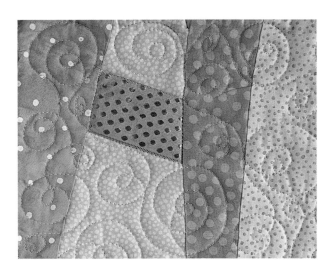

14. Repeat for the remaining eight block 1 patterns and the nine block 2 patterns.

15. When all the blocks are complete, trim the fabric edges with a rotary cutter to the solid line. The dashed line is the stitching line. The blocks should measure 7" x 8½".

16. Leave the paper on the blocks until the blocks are sewn together and the borders are added. Then carefully tear away and discard the paper backing.

Assembling the Quilt

1. Arrange the blocks in six rows of three across. Refer to the quilt diagram or arrange the blocks to your liking. Number each block if desired.

2. Sew each row of blocks together, using the block numbers for reference. Press seams in the opposite direction from row to row. Sew the rows together. Press.

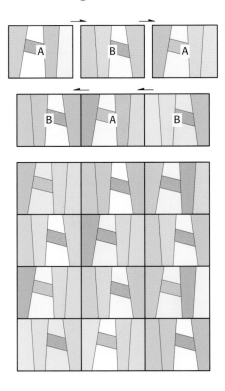

3. Add the petals to create an inner border. Align the petals with the edge of the blocks, slightly overlapping them. Baste or pin the petals in place. You can machine baste them with a scant ¼" seam. The stitching will be enclosed in the ¼" seam when the borders are attached.

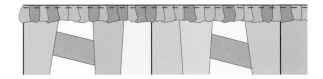

4. Referring to "Adding Borders" on page 16, measure the length of the quilt top through the center and cut the 7" x 42" strips to fit. Sew to the sides of the quilt top. Press the seams toward the center of the quilt; the petals will naturally fall toward the border, forming the "inner border" of petals. Measure the width of the quilt and cut the remaining border strips to that length. Sew to the top and bottom. Press.

Quilt diagram

PETAL POWER

Don't worry about touching the petals with a hot iron. They won't melt or be damaged in any way, and nothing will come off onto the iron. These petals, made from a silk by-product, are tough little critters. You can fuse, glue, or sew them onto fabric. They can be washed in the washer and dried in the dryer. Petals can be added to clothing and manipulated into flowers to be used as accents in many different kinds of projects.

Finishing

Refer to "Finishing Your Quilt" on pages 19–21 for details as needed.

1. Prepare the backing. Layer and baste the quilt with batting and backing.

2. Hand or machine quilt in your favorite style. We added rounded swirls and "bubbles" to repeat the roundness of the polka dots.

3. Make and attach the binding.

Another Polka-Dot Express:
On the Bright Side

Here's a bright alternative to the softer pastel floral version. It has an inner border of black fabric and a "split" outer border for an extra jolt of fun. This quilt reminds me of my first train ride when I was three years old. During the long trip, Mom kept me occupied by making wonderful things from Play-Doh. I'll never forget the little plates of food she made with tiny green peas that looked like polka dots on the white plate. I was captivated!

—Jayme

Pieced by Jayme Crow. Machine quilted by Sandy Sims.

Finished size: 40½" x 55½"
Finished block: 6½" x 8"

Materials

Yardage is based on 42"-wide fabric.

- ¾ yard *each* of 2 coordinating fabrics (1 fuchsia and 1 blue) for outer border

- ⅜ yard of black polka-dot fabric for inner border

- 2 fat quarters for blocks (piece A)

- 6 fat quarters for blocks

- 1 fat eighth of black-and-white fabric or scraps for outer-border accent

- 2⅝ yards of fabric for backing

- ½ yard of fabric for binding

- 46" x 61" piece of batting

- 2¼ yards of 1½"-wide polka-dot ribbon

- 4½ yards of ¼"-wide fusible-web tape for attaching ribbon (optional)

Cutting

*All measurements include ¼" seam allowances.
See the fat quarter cutting guides on page 38 before
you cut. You will have some extra pieces to give you
choices when piecing. For the most efficient cutting,
choose two of the fat quarters for the piece A portion
of the blocks; that will be the background for the
ribbons.*

**From *each* of the 2 fat quarters for
piece A, cut:**

5 strips, 4" x 18"; crosscut *each* into 2 pieces,
    4" x 9"

From the polka-dot ribbon, cut:

18 pieces, 4" long

From *each* of the 6 fat quarters, cut:

5 strips, 3" x 18"; crosscut *each* into 2 pieces,
    3" x 9"

**From the black polka-dot inner-border
fabric, cut:**

2 strips, 2" x 39½"

2 strips, 2" x 27½"

From the fuchsia fabric, cut:

3 strips, 7" x 42"; crosscut 1 into:

- 1 piece, 7" x 17¼"
- 1 piece, 7" x 10"

From the blue fabric, cut:

3 strips, 7" x 42"; crosscut 1 into:

- 1 piece, 7" x 17¼"
- 1 piece, 7" x 10"

**From the black-and-white outer-border
accent fabric, cut:**

2 pieces, 1¼" x 7"

From the binding fabric, cut:

5 strips, 2¼" x 40"

Piecing the Blocks

Follow the directions for the floral quilt beginning on page 39 to make 18 blocks.

Assembling the Quilt

1. Follow steps 1 and 2 on page 41. We inverted some blocks for a more random look.

2. Sew a 2" x 39½" black polka-dot strip to each side of the quilt top. Press toward the strips. Sew the 2" x 27½" black polka-dot strips to the top and bottom. Press.

3. Join the fuchsia 7" x 17¼" strip to a 1¼" x 7" black-and-white strip. Join those two pieces to the blue 7" x 10" strip. Repeat with the remaining 7" x 17¼" blue strip, 1¼" x 7" black-and-white strip, and the 7" x 10" fuchsia piece. The finished border strips should measure 7" x 27½". Press the seams toward the accent strip.

4. Sew one pieced border strip across the top of the quilt. Position it so that the long fuchsia piece is to the left edge or side of the quilt, as shown in the photograph on page 43.

5. Measure and sew the remaining pieced border strip to the bottom of the quilt. Place the border strips so that the long blue strip is on the right edge.

6. Measure the quilt from top to bottom through the center; piece two 7" x 42" blue border strips and cut to that measurement. Sew it to the blue side of the quilt. Repeat for the other side border. Finish the quilt as directed on page 42.

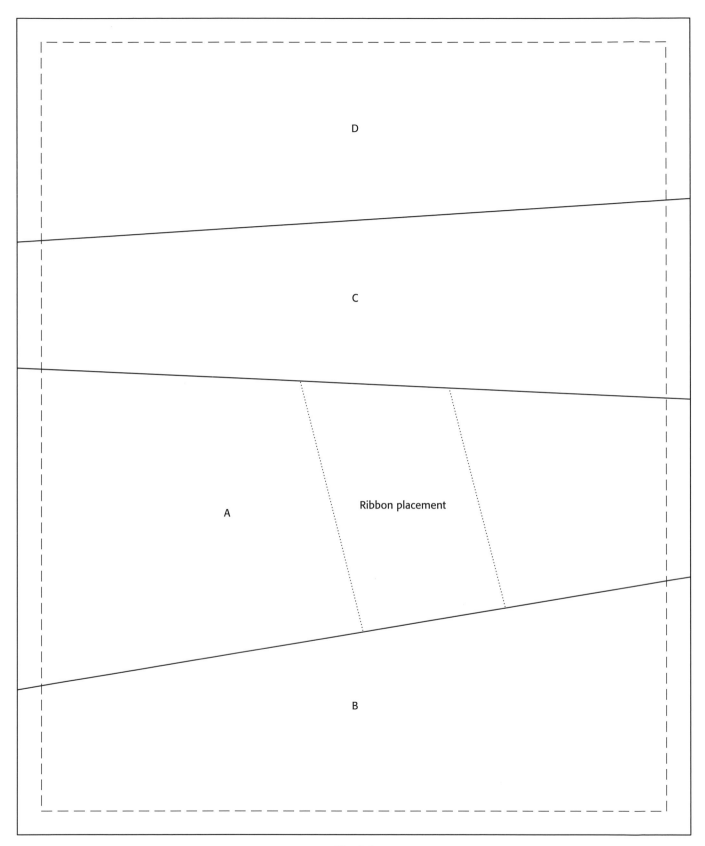

Block 1

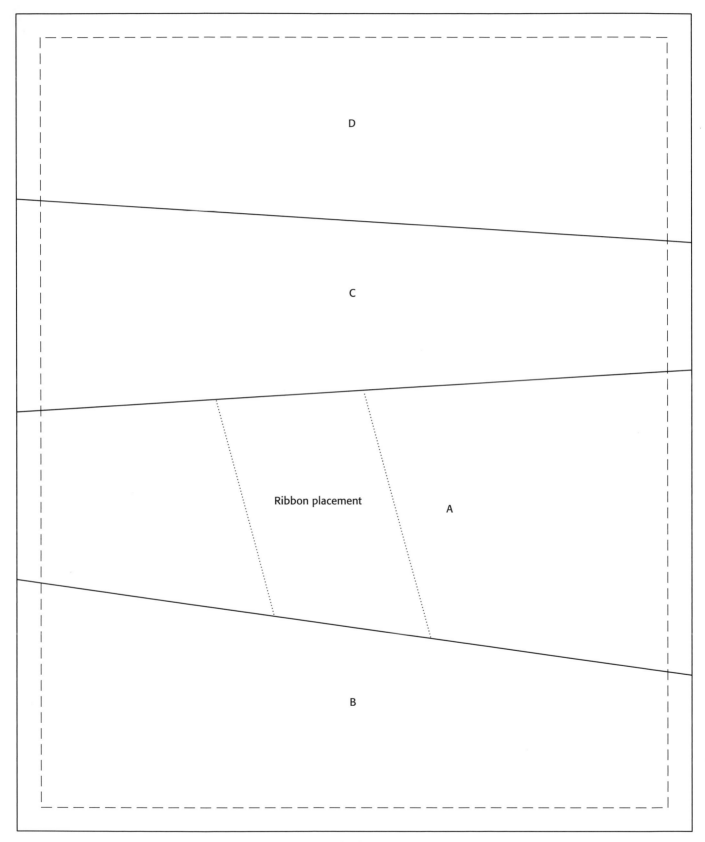

D

C

Ribbon placement

A

B

Block 2

Winter Aspens

My family has a cabin in Colorado, and I love the aspens there at
all times of the year. I designed this wall hanging to instill the calm of
a quiet winter snowfall. Only four fabrics were used for the sky and trees.
It's all about placing dark against light for a dramatic contrast.

—Joan

Pieced and quilted by Joan Segna.

Finished quilt: 26" x 34"

Materials

All yardages are based on 42"-wide fabric.

- ¾ yard of preshrunk muslin for background

- ⅝ yard of black fabric with white polka dots
  for sky

- ⅜ yard of black-and-white print for outer border

- ¼ yard *each of 3* different white fabrics with
  black polka dots for trees

- ¼ yard of white dots on off-white fabric
  for inner border

- ¼ yard of dark blue or purple fabric for
  accent border

- 4 fat eighths *total* of assorted white, off-white,
  and white-on-gray fabrics for foreground

- 1⅛ yards of fabric for backing

- ⅜ yard of fabric for binding

- 32" x 40" piece of batting

- Freezer paper

- Invisible nylon thread

Cutting

All measurements include ¼" seam allowances.

From the preshrunk muslin, cut:

1 rectangle, 20" x 28"

From the black fabric with white polka dots, cut:

1 rectangle, 16½" x 20½"

From the off-white inner-border fabric, cut:

3 strips, 2" x 42"

From the blue or purple accent border fabric, cut:

3 strips, 1¼" x 42"

From the black-and-white outer-border print, cut:

3 strips, 3" x 42"

From the binding fabric, cut:

4 strips, 2¼" x 42"

Preparing the Appliqués

1. Enlarge the diagram on page 53 and draw the nine trees onto freezer paper to make your patterns. You can use ordinary paper or tracing paper for the patterns, but freezer paper will help stabilize the long, narrow pieces of fabric before they are appliquéd to the background.

2. Cut three trees from each of the three white fabrics with black polka dots. Press the freezer-paper templates to the wrong side of the fabric and cut around them, leaving ¼" for seam allowances.

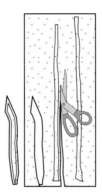

When cutting the trees, remember:
- Add ¼" on all sides.
- The base of the tree should be wider than the top.
- Curves and irregularities are desirable—nature is not perfect. Wiggles and knots are good. You don't want your trees to look like fence posts!
- Use smaller dots for smaller trees in the background.
- Use larger, more defined dots for larger trees in the foreground.

3. Make freezer-paper templates from foreground patterns 1–7. Mark the top and bottom on the paper templates. Press to the wrong side of the fabrics for the foreground and cut the following pieces, leaving ¼" around the templates for seam allowances:
   - Pieces 1 and 2 from one fat eighth
   - Pieces 3 and 4 from a second fat eighth
   - Pieces 5 and 6 from a third fat eighth
   - Piece 7 from the fourth fat eighth

Assembling the Quilt

1. Press the 20" x 28" preshrunk muslin background piece. On the right side of the fabric, use a pencil and ruler to draw a 16" x 24" rectangle in the center. Extend the lines at the corners beyond the measurement as shown. Draw a second set of lines ¼" beyond the first lines.

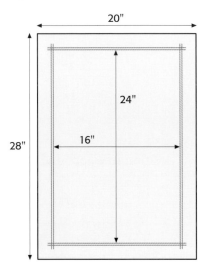

2. Press the quilt backing fabric and lay it right side down. Lay the batting on top and smooth out any wrinkles. Center the muslin background on top, right side up, so that the drawn lines are visible. Do not trim the excess batting and backing; the borders will be sewn on later.

3. Press the 16½" x 20½" black fabric with white polka dots and place it on the muslin background fabric using the outer lines on the top and sides of the muslin as a guide. Press again to help the fabric "grip" the muslin and keep it stable. Pin in place.

4. Select tree appliqué 1. Press under ¼" on each long edge. Remember: Wiggles and curves are good. Remove the freezer paper.

Position the tree so that the bottom edge matches the bottom of the sky fabric and the right edge is approximately 4" from the first line drawn on the muslin background. Pin in place.

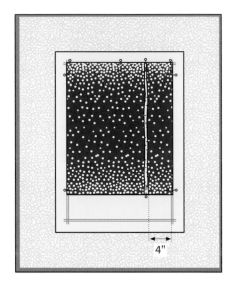

5. Refer to "Machine Appliqué" on page 14. Thread your machine with invisible thread, use an open-toe embroidery foot, and select the blind hem stitch on your machine.

6. Start at the bottom inside edge of the tree and appliqué with the blind hem stitch, first one side and then the other side. Sew through all layers.

7. Select foreground pieces 1 and 2. Turn under ¼" on the top edge and press to the wrong side. Remove the freezer paper. Position foreground piece 1 on the left-hand side of the quilt top, up about 6" from the bottom, matching the outside edge to the outside line drawn on the muslin background. Position piece 2 on the right-hand side, up 5" from the bottom, matching the outside edge to the outer drawn line. The

pieces should overlap the sky fabric by ¼".
When properly placed, pin in position and
blind hem stitch the pressed edges.

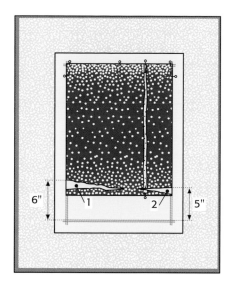

8. Turn under ¼" on the top edge of foreground piece 3 and press the seam allowance. Remove the freezer paper and position
piece 3 along the left edge, below piece 1.
Appliqué in place with a blind hem stitch.

9. Press under ¼" on the top edge of foreground piece 4. Remove the freezer paper
and position it between pieces 1 and 2.
Pin in place and blind hem stitch the
pressed edge.

10. Select tree appliqué 2. Fold each side
edge under ¼" to the wrong side and
press. Remove the freezer paper. Match the
bottom edge of the tree with the bottom
edge of foreground piece 3, approximately
1½" from the inner line on the left side of
the muslin background piece. Pin in place
and appliqué with a blind hem stitch from
bottom to top on both sides.

11. Select tree appliqués 3, 4, and 5 for the
grouping of trees on the far right side of
quilt. Turn and press the edges under ¼";
remove the freezer paper. Match the tree
bottoms to the bottom edge of foreground
piece 4. Position tree appliqué 3 behind 4.
Trees 3 and 4 should be approximately 1¾"
from the inner line on the right edge. Tree
5 should be 2½" from the edge. Appliqué
each tree in place.

12. Select foreground piece 5. Fold the top edge
under ¼" and press. Remove the freezer
paper and position on the quilt top. The left
edge should line up with the outer line on

the left side of the muslin background. Pin in place and appliqué.

13. Select foreground piece 6; turn under the top edge ¼" and press. Remove the freezer paper and position at the base of the three grouped trees. Pin in place and appliqué.

14. Select tree appliqués 6 and 7. Turn under ¼" along the edges and press; remove the freezer paper. Position with the bottom edges of the trees parallel to the bottom edge of foreground piece 5; the left edge of tree 6 should be approximately 2½" from the inner line on the left edge of the muslin background. Pin in place and appliqué. Pin tree 7 next to tree 6. The base of tree 7 can slightly overlap the base of tree 6.

15. Select foreground piece 7. Turn under ¼" along the top edge and press; remove the freezer paper. Position at the bottom of the quilt. The side and bottom edges should overlap to the outer drawn line. Pin in place and appliqué.

16. Select tree appliqués 8 and 9. Turn under ¼" along the sides and press; remove the freezer paper. Position in place. The bottom edges should be positioned along the bottom outer line and approximately 5½" and 7" from the right inner line. Pin in place and appliqué.

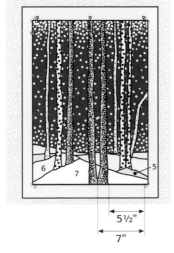

Finishing

The center of the quilt will be quilted before the borders are added. The quilting may move the quilt top around slightly and produce some wiggly edges. You will have crisper, straighter borders if they are added last. When you add the borders to the quilt, you will be both sewing and quilting through all layers.

1. See the quilt diagram on page 53 for suggested quilting lines. Use a walking foot for quilting if you have one. Use quilting stitches to add contour lines to the hills and foreground and a few "random" clouds in the sky.

2. Square up the quilt by using your ruler to draw a chalk line all around the edges. Use the chalk line as a guide for sewing the borders. Refer to "Squaring Up" on page 17.

3. Refer to "Adding Borders" on page 16. Measure and sew an off-white inner-border strip to each side, sewing through all layers. Sew inner borders to the top and bottom.

4. Measure and sew a blue or purple accent border to each side of the quilt.

5. Measure and sew the accent border to the top and bottom of the quilt.

6. Measure and sew the 3" outer-border strips to each side of the quilt. Measure and sew outer borders to the top and bottom.

7. Add additional quilting lines or designs to the borders if desired.

8. Refer to "Binding" on page 20 to make and add binding to your quilt.

Pattern is reversed for fusible appliqué.   Enlarge pattern 250%.   - - Quilting line

Summer Sailing

I've always loved impressionist paintings. Everything you need to see is there in light sketchy strokes and dots. Like the dots that shape these paintings, the dots of experience, people, and family in our lives organize to make us who we are. I've used my dotted fabric to create this peaceful and serene boating scene. It is a seemingly haphazard collection of dots that all come together into a warm, sunny day.

—Joan

Pieced and quilted by Joan Segna.

Finished quilt: 37½" x 31½"

Materials

Yardage is based on 42"-wide fabric. Refer to the diagram on page 59 for piece numbers.

- 1 yard of preshrunk muslin for quilt background
- ¾ yard of yellow dotted fabric for foreground (piece 10) and binding
- ½ yard of grayish blue for lower sky (piece 3)
- ⅜ yard of green fabric for outer border
- ⅜ yard of light blue fabric for middle sky (piece 2)
- ⅜ yard of yellowish green fabric for shoreline (piece 9)
- ¼ yard of medium blue fabric for upper sky (piece 1)
- ¼ yard of light blue fabric for water in foreground (piece 8)
- ¼ yard of light beige fabric for distant hills (piece 4)
- ¼ yard of medium green fabric for immediate foreground (piece 12)
- ¼ yard of orange fabric for inner border
- 1 fat quarter of multicolored fabric for foreground (piece 11)
- 1 fat quarter of brown fabric for tree
- ⅛ yard of medium grayish blue fabric for water (piece 7)
- 1 fat eighth of medium beige fabric for hills (piece 5)
- 1 fat eighth of green fabric for hills (piece 6)

- 3 pieces, 9" x 9", of assorted green fabrics for tree leaves
- 1 piece, 8" x 8", of white fabric for sails
- 1 piece, 5" x 9", of brown fabric for boat masts
- 1 piece, 3" x 8", of white fabric for large sailboat
- 2 pieces, 3" x 6", of coordinating colors for small boats
- 3 pieces, 2" x 9", for boat stripes
- 1¼ yards of fabric for backing
- 38" x 44" piece of batting
- 3 sheets of 9" x 12" fusible web
- Invisible nylon thread

ADDING GLITZ

I used dupioni silk for the orange and green borders. It's optional, but it added a nice bit of shine and shimmer to frame the sailboat scene.

Cutting

All measurements include ¼" seam allowances.

From the muslin, cut:
1 rectangle, 28" x 34"

From the orange fabric, cut:
3 strips, 1½" x 42"

From the green outer-border fabric, cut:
4 strips, 2½" x 42"

From the binding fabric, cut:
4 strips, 2¼" x 42"

Preparing the Appliqués

1. On a large sheet of paper, draw a 25" x 31" rectangle. We recommend flip-chart paper that has a grid of 1" blue squares printed on it. Use the pattern diagram on page 59 as a guide to draw the 11 lines that form the sky, hills, water, and foreground. The lines do not need to be exact or match the diagram precisely; you will make your own pattern and work from that. Note that piece 7 creates the horizon line, so the top edge needs to be a straight horizontal line.

2. When you are satisfied with your drawing, number the pieces as shown in the diagram and cut your paper apart along the lines to make the 12 pattern pieces.

3. Use each pattern piece to cut the appropriate fabric. As you cut each piece, remember to add a minimum ¼" seam allowance on all sides.

4. Use the patterns on pages 60 and 61 to trace the boats, sails, and masts onto the paper side of the fusible web.

5. Use the patterns on pages 62 and 63 to trace the tree trunk, branches, and leaves onto the paper side of the fusible web.

6. Following the manufacturer's instructions, iron the fusible web to the wrong side of the chosen fabrics. Cut out the traced shapes on the drawn lines.

Assembling the Quilt

1. Place the pressed backing fabric face down. Place the batting on top. Center the 28" x 34" pressed and preshrunk muslin background fabric on top of the batting and backing.

2. Press all three layers and pin together. Do not trim the excess batting and backing fabric. The inner and outer borders will be sewn on later.

3. On the muslin background fabric, draw the 25" x 31" rectangle to establish your outer boundaries.

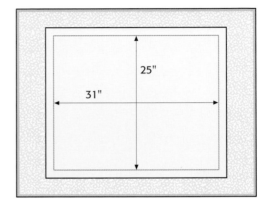

4. Referring to the diagram on page 59, start with piece 1, the upper sky, in the upper right-hand corner. Pin the fabric in place, overlapping the outer boundary by ¼".

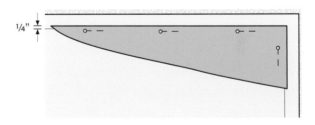

5. Press the upper edge of piece 2 under ¼" following the cut curves. Align the piece ¼" beyond the right edge boundary line, overlapping piece 1 by ¼". Pin in place.

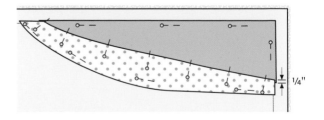

6. Refer to "Machine Appliqué" on page 14. With monofilament thread, a large needle, and your machine set to appropriate blind-hem-stitch width, sew along the top folded edge of piece 2, just catching the edge of piece 2. Stitch through all four layers (piece 1, muslin, batting, and backing).

7. Follow the diagram on the opposite page, and in numerical order, continue to press under, pin in place, and blind hem stitch the upper folded edge of each piece. Be sure that the top edge of piece 7 is straight, since it creates the horizon line.

Finishing

The center of the quilt will be quilted before borders are added. The quilting may move the quilt top around slightly and produce some wiggly edges. You will have crisper, straighter borders if they are added last. When you add the borders to the quilt, you will be both sewing and quilting through all layers. We also found it easier to quilt before adding the fusible appliqués. Don't quilt as heavily in the areas where the appliqués will go.

1. Follow the quilt diagram at right for suggested quilting lines. Use a walking foot for quilting if you have one. As you quilt, add contour lines to the hills and foreground, and ripples in the water.

2. Refer to the quilt diagram at right to fuse the tree and leaves to the left side of quilt.

3. Fuse stripes to the boats; then fuse the masts, sails, and boats to the quilt.

4. Square up the quilt by using your ruler to draw a chalk line all around the edges. Use the chalk line as a guide for sewing the borders. Refer to "Squaring Up" on page 17.

5. Refer to "Adding Borders" on page 16. Sew a side inner border to each side. Sew inner borders to the top and bottom.

6. Add additional quilting lines or designs to the borders, if desired.

7. Refer to "Binding" on page 20 to make and add binding to your quilt.

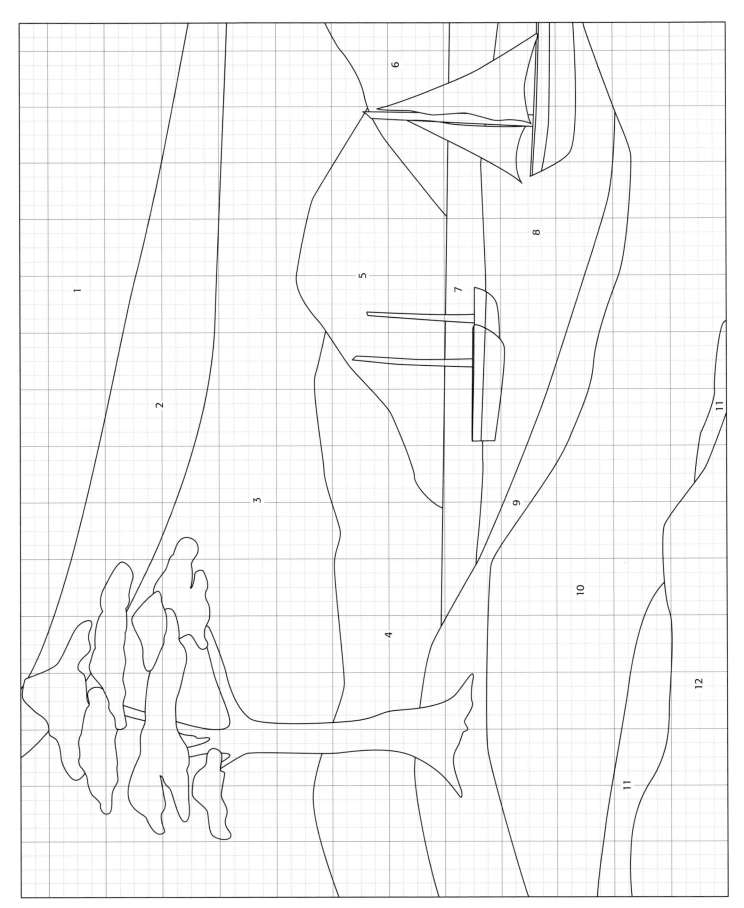

Pattern diagram
Enlarge pattern 340%.

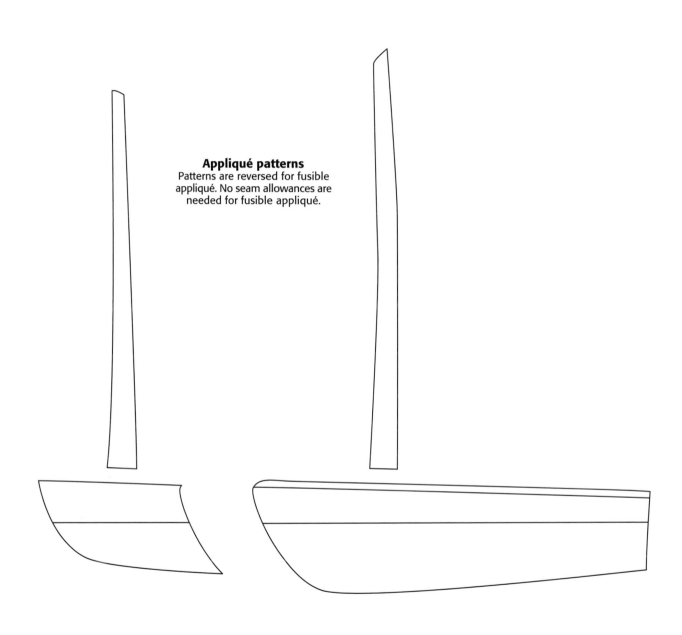

Appliqué patterns
Patterns are reversed for fusible
appliqué. No seam allowances are
needed for fusible appliqué.

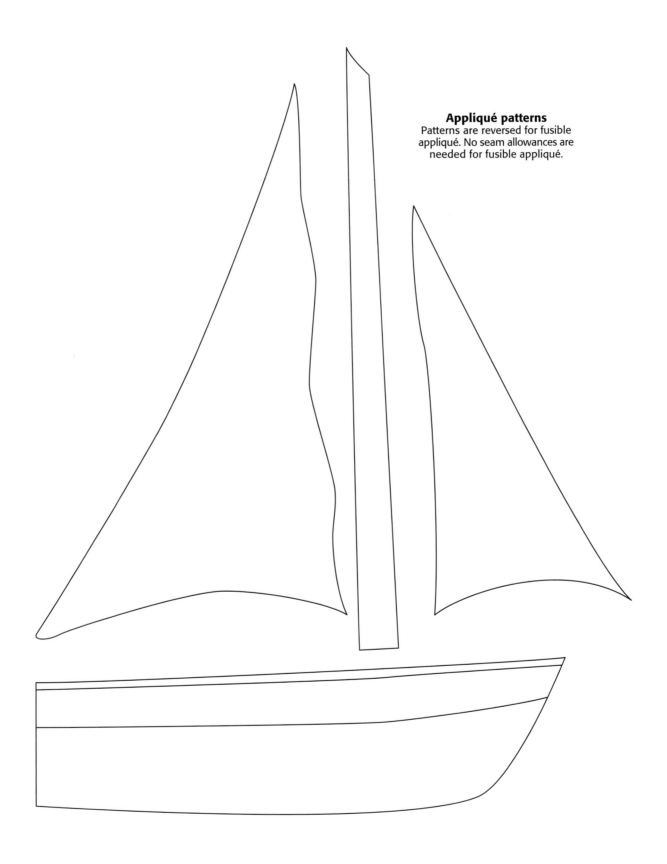

Appliqué patterns
Patterns are reversed for fusible appliqué. No seam allowances are needed for fusible appliqué.

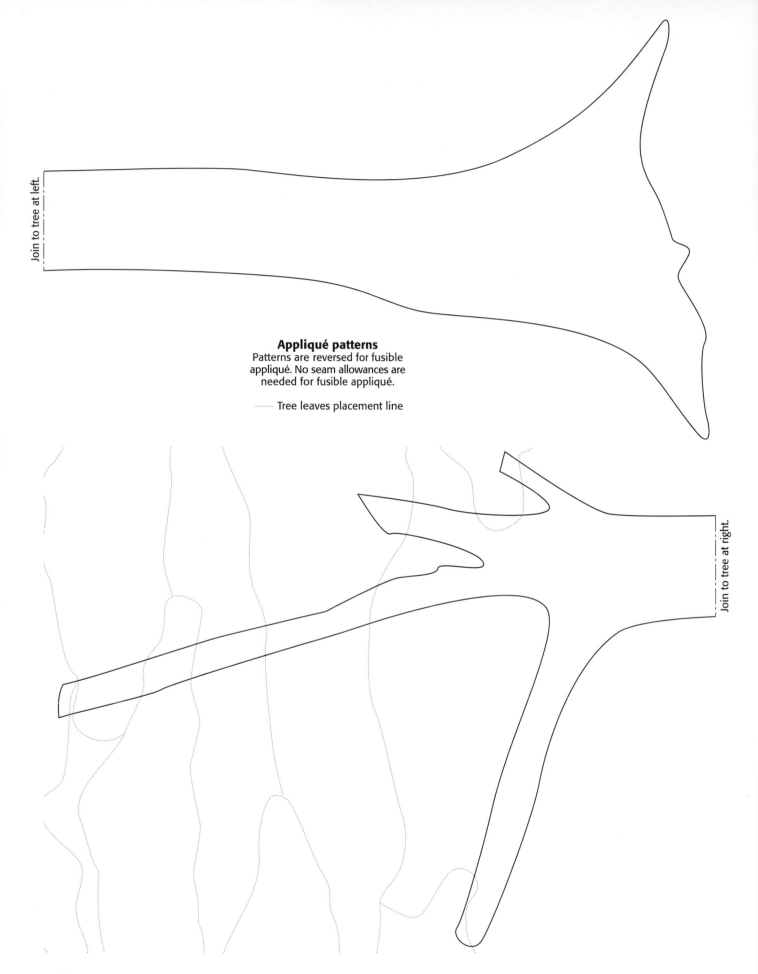

Join to tree at left.

Appliqué patterns
Patterns are reversed for fusible
appliqué. No seam allowances are
needed for fusible appliqué.

········· Tree leaves placement line

Join to tree at right.

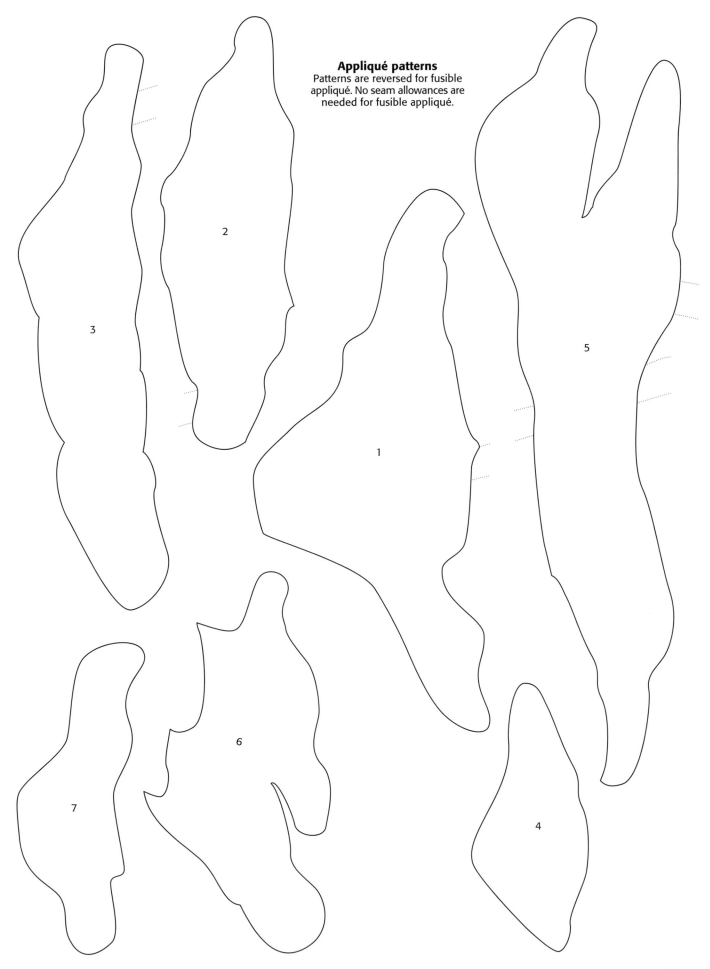

Appliqué patterns
Patterns are reversed for fusible
appliqué. No seam allowances are
needed for fusible appliqué.

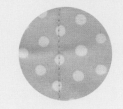

Salon Grotto

An afternoon at a spa is an indulgence. That's how I view this quilt—
a quilter's afternoon of relaxation and creativity. Take time out to play with
color and fabrics. Treat yourself to sewing, cutting, and embellishing figures
that remind you of your aunt, mother, grandmother, or best friends. It's fast,
fun, and reminiscent of cutting paper dolls. Imagine the relaxing atmosphere
of a spa as you work; indulge yourself!

—Joan

Pieced and machine quilted by Joan Segna.

Finished quilt: 24" x 27"

Materials

All yardages are based on 42"-wide fabric unless otherwise noted. Refer to the diagram on page 70 for panel numbers. See "Designing with Dots" on page 8 for a discussion of fabrics used in this quilt.

- ⅝ yard of white or off-white fabric for background

- ½ yard of light fabric for outer border

- ¼ yard of gold-and-white striped fabric for inner border

- ¼ yard of purple fabric for accent border

- 1 fat quarter of dark polka-dot fabric for sofa

- 1 fat eighth of taupe or off-white polka-dot fabric for back wall panel 4

- 1 piece, 8" x 10", *each* of blue, white, and rust fabrics for dresses

- 1 piece, 8" x 10", *each* of purple and brown fabric for pillows

- 1 piece, 8" x 10", of brown for floor

- 1 piece, 8" x 10", *each* of three taupe or off-white polka-dot prints for wall panels 1, 2, and 3

- 1 piece, 8" x 10", of flesh-tone fabric for arms/hands and faces

- 1 piece, 7" x 8", *each* of two different fabrics for stockings

- 1 piece, 4" x 6", *each* of gold, red, and brown fabrics for hair

- 1 piece, 4" x 4", *each* of red, blue, and white polka-dot fabrics for shoes

- 3 yards of 1"-wide ruffled organdy ribbon

- 1⅛ yards of fabric for backing

- ⅜ yard of fabric for binding

- 30" x 33" piece of batting

- 3 sheets, 9" x 12", of lightweight fusible web

- 1 permanent fine-tipped marker in light red

- 1 permanent fine-tipped marker in black

- Invisible nylon thread

- Decorative threads

Cutting

All measurements include ¼" seam allowances.

From the gold-and-white striped fabric, cut:
2 strips, 2" x 42"

From the purple fabric, cut:
2 strips, 1¼" x 42"

From the light outer-border fabric, cut:
3 strips, 3½" x 42"

From the binding fabric, cut:
3 strips, 2¼" x 42"

Preparing the Appliqués

The illustration below shows placement for the wall panels, sofa, and floor.

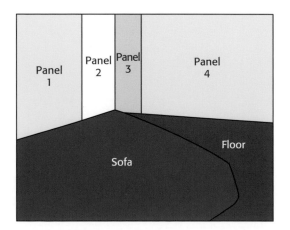

1. **Wall Panel 1.** Cut a 4½" x 8¼" rectangle.

2. **Wall Panel 2.** Cut a 2½" x 7½" rectangle.

3. **Wall Panel 3.** Cut a 2¼" x 7" rectangle.

4. **Wall Panel 4.** Cut a 7" x 8¾" rectangle.

5. **Sofa.** Cut a 7½" x 14½" rectangle. Measure 8" from the left across the top and make a mark. Measure 5½" up the left side and make a mark. Draw a line between the two marks and cut along that line. Measure 4" up on the right side and make a mark. Draw a line from that mark to your first 8" mark on the top, and cut along that line.

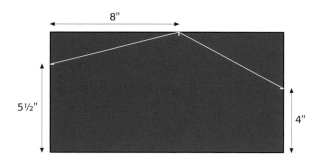

6. Trace the sofa cutting guide on page 73 onto a piece of paper and then cut out the template. Pin it to the right side of the sofa rectangle, matching the bottom edge to the bottom of the rectangle; the tip should touch the right edge. Cut around the curve, along the diagonal line, and straight up as shown.

7. **Floor.** Cut one 4¾" x 6¾" rectangle.

8. Trace the two pillow patterns on page 73 onto paper to make templates. Cut out one purple pillow and one brown pillow, adding ¼" all around the template for seam allowances.

9. The remainder of the appliqué pieces will be fused in place. Follow the manufacturer's instructions for the fusible web and trace the patterns on pages 71 and 72 onto the paper side of the fusible web with at least ½" between pieces. Trace the following: blue dress; white dress; rust dress; gold hair; red hair; brown hair; four arms/hands; three stockings; three faces; and red, blue, and white shoes. Cut out each piece ¼" beyond the drawn lines and fuse to the wrong side of the chosen fabrics. Cut on the solid lines and set the pieces aside.

Note: The solid lines are cutting lines; dashed lines indicate stitching lines for quilting.

ADDING CHARACTER

In the figures, the stitching lines are important. They add form and attitude, bestowing your people with personality. Use a light pencil to draw them on.

Assembling the Quilt

1. Press the background fabric and trim it to 18" x 22". With the fabric positioned as shown and right side up, use a pencil to draw a 13" x 16" rectangle. Extend the lines

out an inch or so on both ends. Draw a second set of lines ¼" beyond the first lines.

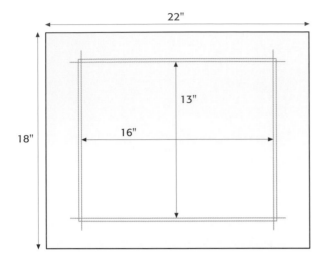

2. Press the backing fabric. Lay it right side down, add the batting, and center the marked background on top, right side up, so that the drawn lines are visible. Do not trim the excess batting and backing; the borders will be sewn on later.

3. Place panel 1 on the quilt background, matching edges to the outer lines. Pin in place.

4. With right sides together, place panel 2 on top of panel 1, aligning the edges as shown. Pin in place and sew together, through all

layers, using a ¼" seam allowance. Remove the pins. Open the piece and press.

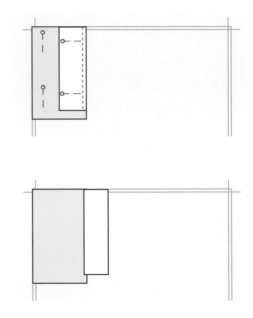

5. Place panel 3 on top of panel 2, with right sides together and aligning the edges. Sew a ¼" seam through all layers. Open and press.

6. Repeat the procedure for panel 4. Press the panels.

7. Position the floor panel, matching edges with the outer lines. Flip it up to align with panel 4. Pin and sew together using a ¼" seam allowance. Flip down and press.

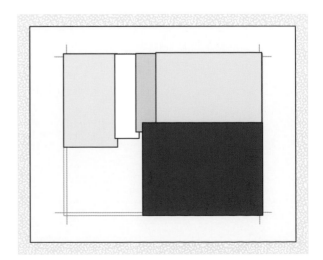

8. **Sofa.** Fold the top edge under ¼" and fold under along the right side where indicated; press. Position the sofa piece on the background, matching the bottom and left edges to the outer pencil line. Referring to "Machine Appliqué" on page 14, use an open-toe embroidery foot, invisible thread, and a blind hem stitch to sew along the folded edge. Sew through all layers. Press the sofa and floor piece.

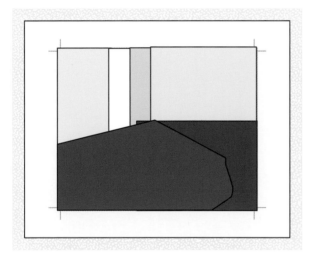

9. Select the purple pillow (piece 1); turn under ¼" along the top, right side, and bottom. Press. Follow the quilt diagram on page 70 to position the purple pillow, matching the unfolded left edge to the outer pencil line on the quilt background. Sew the pressed edges using invisible thread and the blind hem stitch.

10. Referring to the quilt diagram on page 70, position the lady in the white dress, her face, hair, hand, and shoes (pattern pieces 2, 3, 4, 5, and 6). Peel the backing paper from all the pieces and, when they are placed properly, adhere with an iron.

11. Fold under ¼" along the top and bottom edges of the brown pillow (piece 7), except where indicated on the pattern. Refer to the quilt diagram to position the pillow. Pin in place and sew along the folded edges with the blind hem stitch.

12. Select the pieces for the lady in the blue dress (pieces 8 through 15). Peel off the paper backing and arrange the pieces on the quilt. When properly positioned, adhere with an iron.

13. Peel the paper backing from the pieces for the lady in the rust dress (pieces 16 through 21). Place the pieces on the quilt using the outside line as a guide. When properly positioned, adhere with an iron.

Quilting

The center of the quilt will be quilted before borders are added. Change to a walking foot, if you have one, or a regular presser foot. Refer to the dashed stitching lines on the quilt diagram and templates. These are the quilting lines; they give form and dimension to each object as well as hold the layers together. Change thread color for each different fabric color. If you are comfortable with free-motion machine quilting, use a darning foot and do the stitching free motion.

1. Begin by stitching the panels in the center and work outward.

2. Follow the dashed lines to quilt the sofa and pillows.

3. Stitch dashed lines for each figure and stitch around the clothing for added depth.

4. Sew accent stitches in the hair.

Finishing

1. Square up the quilt by using your ruler to draw a chalk line all around the edges. Use the chalk line as a guide for sewing the borders. Refer to "Squaring Up" on page 17.

2. Refer to "Adding Borders" on page 16. Measure the quilt and sew the inner border to each side of the quilt, stitching through all layers. Press. Measure and sew the inner border to the top and bottom. Press.

3. Measure and sew accent borders to the sides first and then to the top and bottom.

4. Repeat the procedure to sew outer borders to the sides first and then to the top and bottom.

5. Trim the backing and batting even with the outside border edges.

6. Add ribbon to the quilt. You can either sew it on or use ½" strips of regular fusible web. Adhere or stitch the ribbon to the outer border, ¼" from the quilt edge. We chose fusible web because of the "architectural" look it gave.

7. Add additional quilting lines or designs to the borders if desired.

8. Refer to "Binding" on page 20 to make and add binding to your quilt.

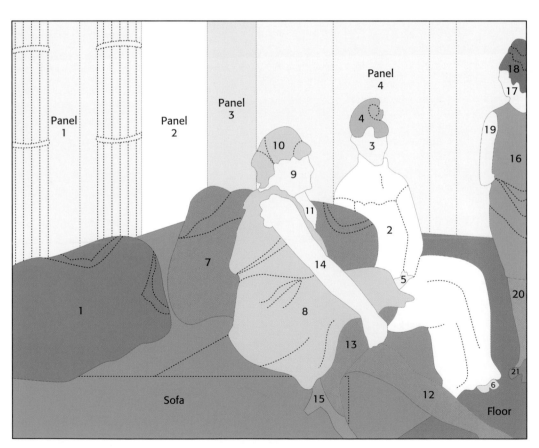

Quilting line ······

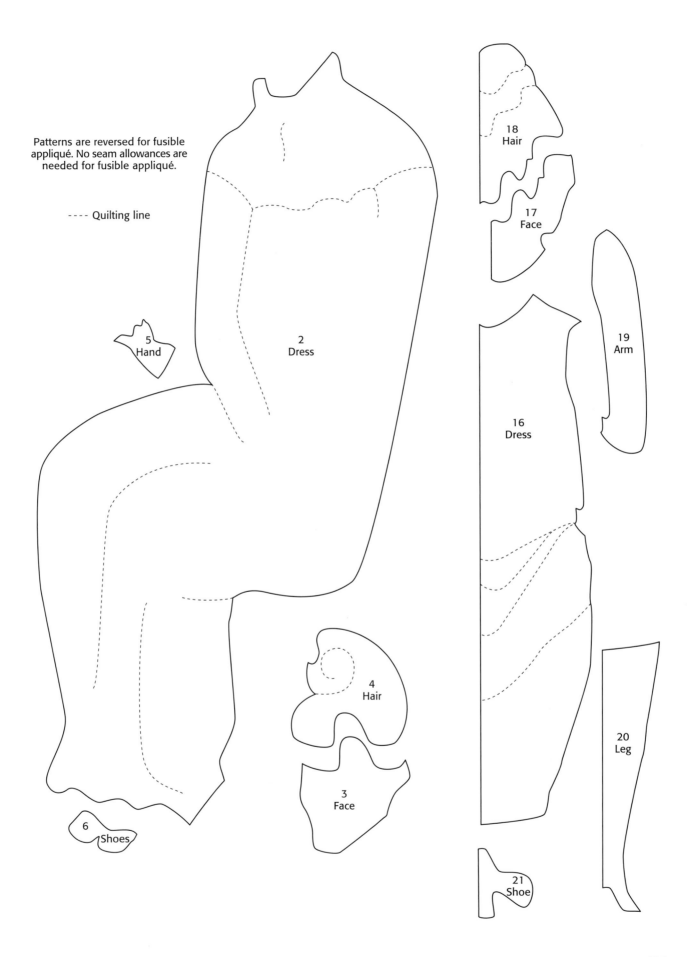

Patterns are reversed for fusible
appliqué. No seam allowances are
needed for fusible appliqué.

- - - - Quilting line

18
Hair

17
Face

5
Hand

2
Dress

19
Arm

16
Dress

4
Hair

3
Face

20
Leg

6
Shoes

21
Shoe

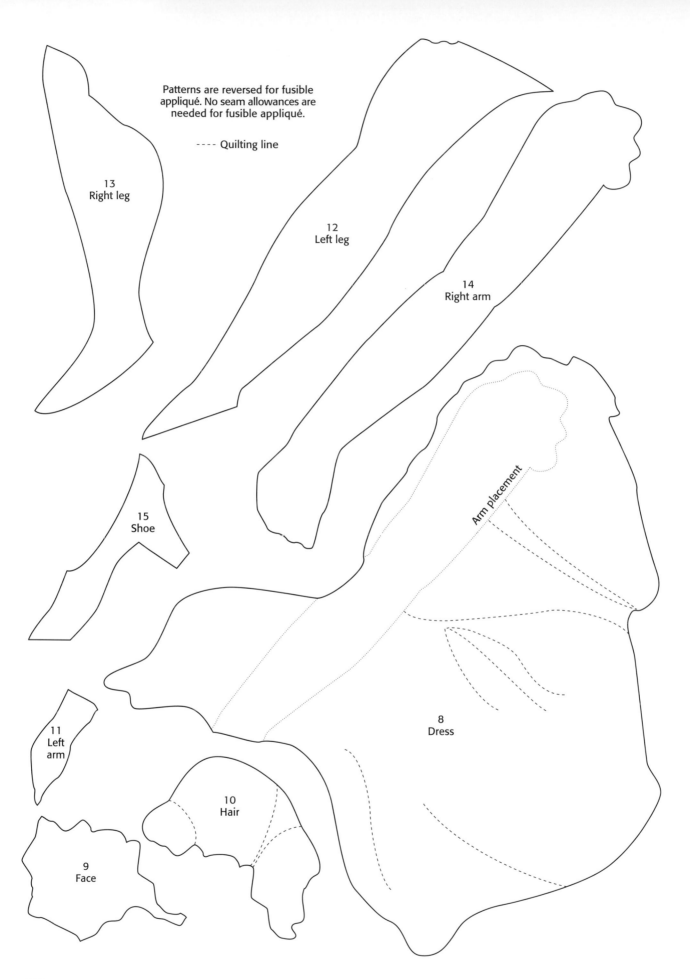

Patterns are reversed for fusible
appliqué. No seam allowances are
needed for fusible appliqué.

---- Quilting line

13
Right leg

12
Left leg

14
Right arm

15
Shoe

Arm placement

8
Dress

11
Left
arm

10
Hair

9
Face

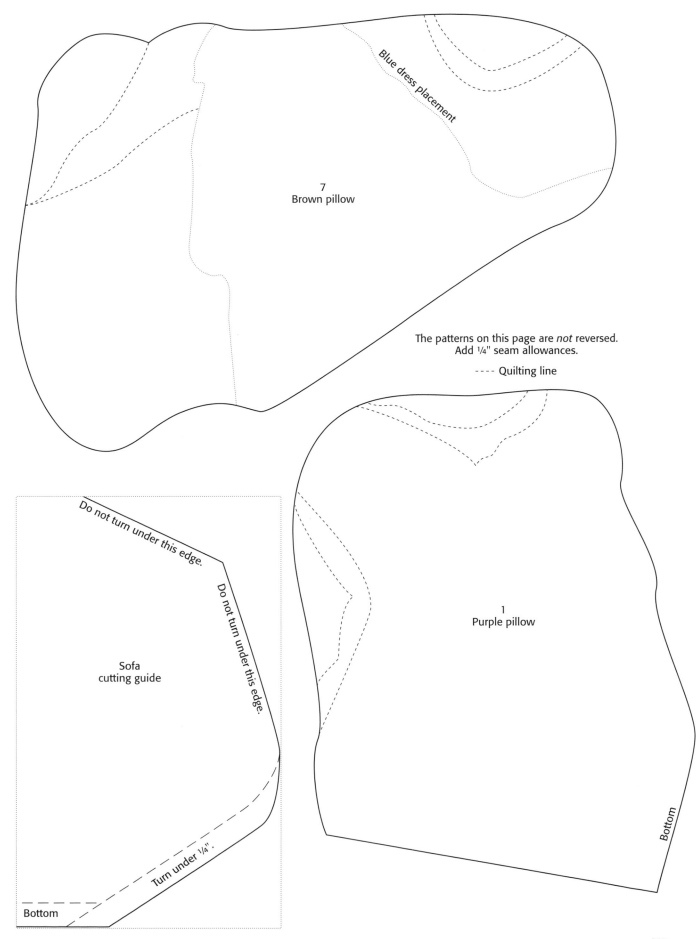

7
Brown pillow

Blue dress placement

The patterns on this page are *not* reversed.
Add ¼" seam allowances.

- - - - Quilting line

Do not turn under this edge.

Do not turn under this edge.

Sofa
cutting guide

Turn under ¼".

Bottom

1
Purple pillow

Bottom

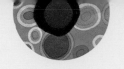

Mega Dots

This is a clever and spirited quilt. The bold primary polka dots are the whimsical dots you expect; I've also added a sprinkling of non-polka-dot fabric, but made the fabric itself a dot by appliquéing it on in the shape of a circle. Watch out, dots come in all sizes and from unexpected places!

—Jayme

Pieced by Jayme Crow. Machine quilted by Sandy Sims.

Finished quilt: 34" x 41½"
Finished block: 7½" x 7½"

75

Materials

Yardage is based on 42"-wide fabric.

- ⅞ yard of fabric for border
- ⅜ yard *each* of 3 coordinating fabrics for block backgrounds
- 12 different fabrics, 6½" x 6½" each, for extra-large dots
- 4 different fabrics, 5½" x 5½" each, for large dots
- 4 different fabrics, 4½" x 4½" each, for medium dots
- 4 different fabrics, 3½" x 3½" each, for small dots
- 4 different fabrics, 3" x 3" each, for tiny dots
- 1½ yards of fabric for backing
- ⅜ yard of fabric for binding
- 40" x 48" piece of batting
- Freezer paper
- Hand-appliqué needles
- Thread to match dot fabrics

Cutting

All measurements include ¼" seam allowances.

From *each* of the three coordinating block background fabrics, cut:
4 squares, 9" x 9" (12 total)

From the border fabric, cut:
4 strips, 6" x 42"

From the binding fabric, cut:
4 strips, 2¼" x 42"

Preparing the Appliqués

1. Using the dot patterns on page 79, trace dots onto freezer paper. Note that we drew some of our dots so they are not perfectly round, to add a little whimsy. Feel free to vary the sizes of the large, medium, small, and tiny dots. You may not use all the circles that you cut; we've included a couple extra to give you more options. On the dull side of the freezer paper, trace 12 extra-large dots and 4 each of the large, medium, small, and tiny dots.

2. Cut out the traced paper dots. Place the shiny side of a freezer-paper dot on the wrong side of the chosen fabric square and iron in place. Repeat the process for all the dots.

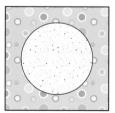

3. Carefully trim the fabric from around each freezer-paper pattern, leaving ¼" of fabric all around for the seam allowance.

4. Press the ¼" seam allowance of fabric over the freezer-paper dot. You can use a little glue from a fabric glue stick, if desired, to help hold the seam in place. The dot is ready to appliqué.

PRESSING POINTER
To get nice, smooth curves on your circles, press with the tip of the iron and hold the edge of the fabric with an awl so you don't burn your fingers. Or purchase a finger protector called Cool Fingers and wear it to keep your fingers from being burned.

Appliquéing the Blocks

1. Place one extra-large dot in the center of one block background and pin in place.

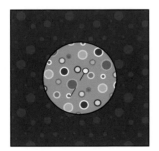

2. Referring to "Hand Appliqué" on page 13, hand stitch the dot to the background block with matching thread. Sew to within 1" of the start of the appliqué seam; carefully pull out the freezer paper and finish appliquéing the dot.

EASY DOT REMOVAL
Use a pair of tweezers to help you remove the freezer-paper dot pattern when the appliqué is nearly complete.

3. Repeat with each extra-large dot, centering, pinning, and hand appliquéing one dot onto the 11 remaining background blocks.

4. Arrange the blocks on a design wall, referring to the quilt diagram on page 78. When satisfied with the layout, number each block to keep track of your layout.

5. While the blocks are still on the design wall, place the large, medium, small, and tiny dots on the extra-large dots. Refer to the photograph on page 74, but use your own judgment. Different fabrics dictate different placement so do what works for your quilt and your fabrics. Rearrange dots until you are satisfied. Offset them here and there, so they have an artistic and pleasing look. Pin all dots in position. Hand appliqué each dot in place.

6. Press the blocks from the wrong side on a terry-cloth towel, to keep the appliqués from squishing flat. Use a rotary cutter and ruler to trim and square the blocks to 8" x 8".

Assembling the Quilt

1. Sew the blocks together in rows, keeping track of the order in your layout. Press the seams in opposite directions from row to row.

2. Sew the rows together and press the seams all in the same direction.

3. Measure the quilt top for borders as instructed in "Adding Borders" on page 16. Cut the side-border strips to the required length and sew them to each side of the quilt. Cut the top and bottom borders to the required length and stitch them to the top and bottom edges of the quilt. Press the seams toward the borders.

Quilt diagram

Finishing

Refer to "Finishing Your Quilt" on pages 19–21 for details as needed.

1. Prepare the backing. Layer and baste the quilt with batting and backing.

2. Hand or machine quilt in your favorite style. Quilt around each of the extra-large dots. Start with the middle dots and work toward each end.

3. Make and attach the binding.

We made this version of "Mega Dots" when the glamorous, sheer dotted material just jumped from the bolt and followed us to the studio—a sophisticated "Mega Dots" was born. See page 10 for a discussion on using dotted sheer fabrics. Pieced by Jayme Crow. Machine quilted by Sandy Sims.

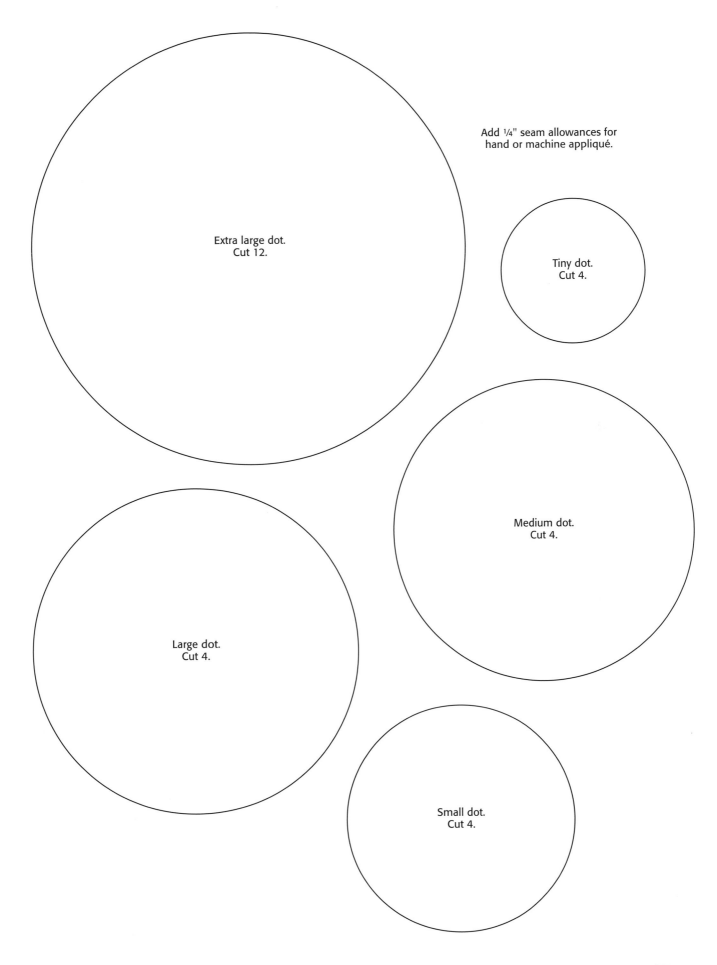

Extra large dot.
Cut 12.

Add ¼" seam allowances for
hand or machine appliqué.

Tiny dot.
Cut 4.

Medium dot.
Cut 4.

Large dot.
Cut 4.

Small dot.
Cut 4.

Daisies Do Tell

Daisies are easy to grow, and they impart a cottage charm to the yard. They are an uncomplicated flower, relaxed and effervescent in their growing. Bouquets of daisies speak to us of down-home country living and Grandma's house. Like the easy-to-grow daisy, this is an easy-to-make quilt. It will bring a smile and remind us of our childhood days, of picking a daisy to find out if "he loves me" or "he loves me not."

—Jayme

Pieced by Jayme Crow. Machine quilted by Sandy Sims.

Finished quilt: 44½" x 54½"
Finished block: 8½" x 11"

Materials

Yardage is based on 42"-wide fabric.

- 2⅛ yards of medium green for background blocks, border, and binding

- 2 yards of light green for background blocks and border

- ½ yard of fabric for stems and inner border

- 16 squares, 9" x 9", for large daisies

- 16 rectangles, 5" x 10", for small inner daisies

- 16 squares, 3" x 3", for daisy centers

- 3 yards of fabric for backing

- 51" x 61" piece of batting

- Template plastic for cutting backgrounds

- 2½ yards of lightweight fusible web

Cutting

All measurements include ¼" seam allowances. Use the patterns on pages 87 and 88 to make templates for the A and B background pieces.

From the inner-border/stem fabric, cut:

5 strips, 1" x 42"

From the remaining inner-border/stem fabric, cut:

16 bias strips, 1¼" x 8"

From the medium green, cut:

16 piece B block backgrounds
3 strips, 5" x 42" (border)
6 strips, 2¼" x 42" (binding)

From the light green, cut:

16 piece A block backgrounds
3 strips, 5" x 42" (border)

Preparing the Appliqués

1. Cut 16 squares, 5" x 5", of fusible web from the large piece. Trace one small inner daisy onto each square using the pattern on page 85.

2. Use the appliqué patterns on pages 85 and 86 to trace 16 large daisies and 16 daisy centers onto the remaining fusible web. Cut out the shapes, leaving at least ¼" all around each piece. Make a stack of large daisies and daisy centers.

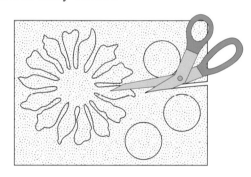

3. Follow the manufacturer's directions and fuse a large, rough-cut daisy to the wrong side of each of the 16 large 9" fabric squares. Cut out each daisy on the drawn lines. Leave the fused paper on and set aside.

4. Cut each 5" x 10" fabric rectangle in half to make two 5" squares. Fuse a 5" square of fusible web with the traced inner daisy to the wrong side of one 5" x 5" square. Remove the paper with the traced daisy and save. Fuse the second 5" square to the first 5" square, wrong sides together. Pin the daisy pattern onto the fused squares. Cut

out along the lines, discard the pattern, and set aside the small inner daisy. Repeat for the remaining 15 inner daisies.

5. Fuse the 16 daisy centers to the wrong side of the 3" x 3" pieces of fabric. Cut out and leave the paper in place. Set aside.

Assembling the Blocks

1. Fold the stem-fabric bias strips in half lengthwise, wrong sides together. Press to form a sharp crease down the center.

2. Place the bias-strip raw edges together on the right side of piece B. Line up the bottom edges; the top of the bias strip should end at the dot on the curve of piece B. Note that it's OK if the raw edge sticks out of the seam. The raw edge will be covered by the daisy.

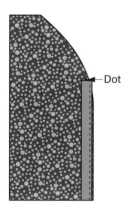

3. Stitch in place ⅛" from the edge to secure the pieces together. The folded edge of the stem should be facing the left edge of piece B.

4. Place piece A onto piece B, right sides together, lining them up at the bottom. Pin in place along the curve and carefully stitch the pieces together from bottom to top

using a ¼" seam. Remove pins. Press the seam toward piece A. You do not need to stitch the other side of the bias stem; it becomes a three-dimensional flower stem. Repeat for the remaining 15 blocks.

5. Peel the paper from the back of one large daisy and position the daisy on a background block, overlapping the top of the stem with the flower. Fuse in place. Repeat for the other 15 daisies.

6. Lay out the blocks and choose one inner daisy and center for each large daisy. When satisfied with the arrangement, take the first small inner daisy and corresponding daisy center from the block. Peel the paper backing from the daisy center and fuse to the small inner daisy. Fuse some of the centers a little off-center to look as if the small daisy is "looking toward the sun" and not staring straight out of the quilt at you! Pin in place on the large daisy. Repeat for the remaining 15 blocks.

7. When all the small inner daisies with centers are pinned in place, adjust a few of them so they are not "dead center" on the large daisies. This makes them more lifelike and interesting.

8. Using a blanket stitch on your sewing machine, stitch around the daisy center onto the large daisy to appliqué it to the block. If your machine does not do a blanket stitch, choose another decorative stitch or use a zigzag stitch. The small inner daisy will be three-dimensional; it is not further stitched to the quilt.

Assembling the Quilt

1. Arrange the blocks in rows of four across and four down. Rearrange them until you are pleased with the placement and overall look. Then sew the blocks together in rows. Sew the rows together to complete the quilt top. Press.

2. Refer to "Adding Borders" on page 16. Measure the center of the quilt from top to bottom. If necessary, join strips to create a piece long enough for this measurement. Cut the inner-border strips to this measurement and sew one strip to each side of the finished quilt top, right sides together. Press seams toward the inner border.

3. Measure through the center of the quilt from side to side, including the inner-border pieces just sewn. Cut two 1" x 42" inner-border pieces to that measurement and sew one to the top and one to the bottom of the quilt, right sides together. Press seams toward the inner border.

4. Repeat the measuring process for the outer borders. Measure from top to bottom; then trim a 5"-wide medium green strip to that length. Sew the strip to the left side of the quilt. Press the seam toward the outer border.

5. Measure the quilt from side to side; then trim a 5" x 42" medium green strip to that measurement. Sew the strip to the bottom of the quilt. Press the seam.

6. Measure the quilt from side to side; then trim a 5" x 42" light green border strip to that measurement. Sew the strip to the top of the quilt. Press the seam.

7. Measure the quilt from top to bottom. Join two pieces of 5" x 42" light green border together and cut a border strip to the correct measurement. Sew to the right side of the quilt. Press the seam.

Finishing

Refer to "Finishing Your Quilt" on pages 19–21 for details as needed.

1. Prepare the backing, piecing it with a horizontal seam. Layer and baste the quilt top with the batting and backing.

2. Hand or machine quilt in your favorite style.

3. Make and attach the binding.

EMBELLISHMENT OPTION

If you have a collection of sparkly beads or jazzy buttons, add them to the flower centers or sprinkle them around the quilt for extra fun.

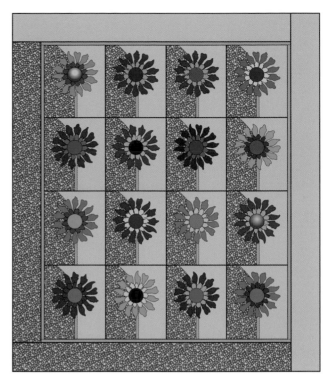

Quilt diagram

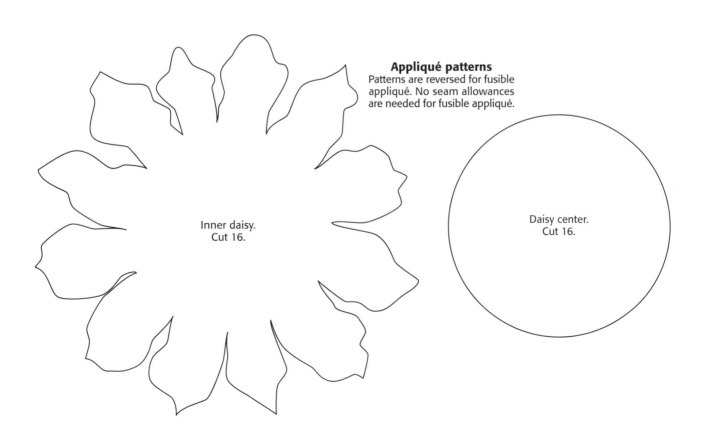

Appliqué patterns
Patterns are reversed for fusible appliqué. No seam allowances are needed for fusible appliqué.

Inner daisy.
Cut 16.

Daisy center.
Cut 16.

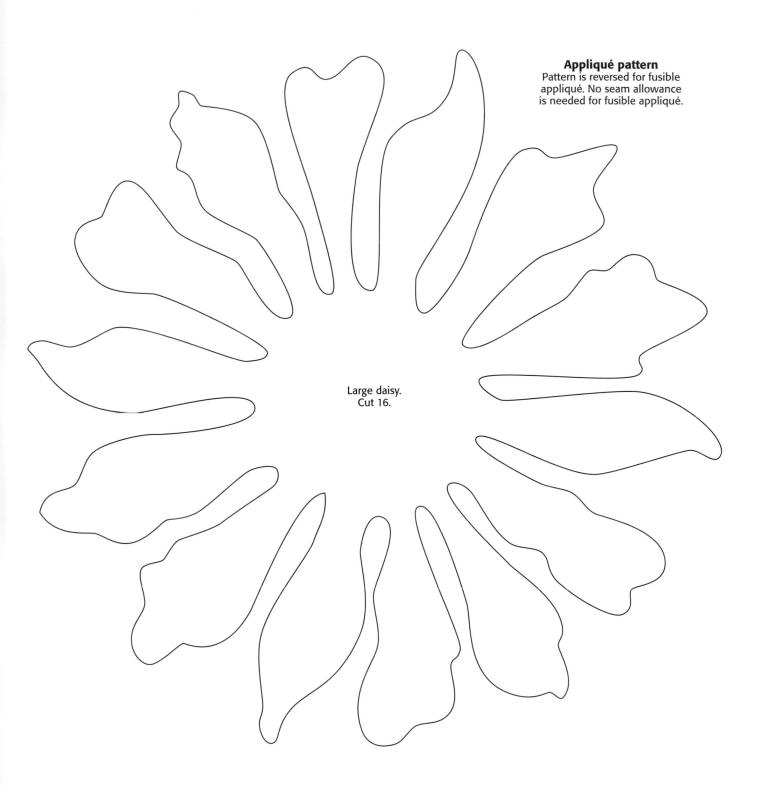

Appliqué pattern
Pattern is reversed for fusible appliqué. No seam allowance is needed for fusible appliqué.

Large daisy.
Cut 16.

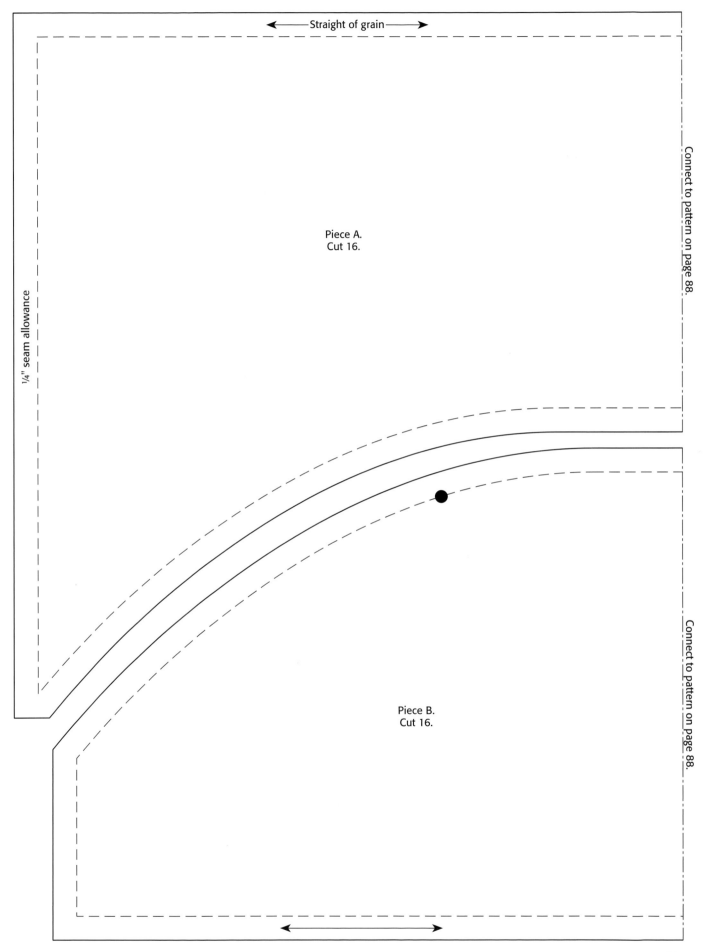

Straight of grain

Piece A.
Cut 16.

¼" seam allowance

Connect to pattern on page 88.

Connect to pattern on page 88.

Piece B.
Cut 16.

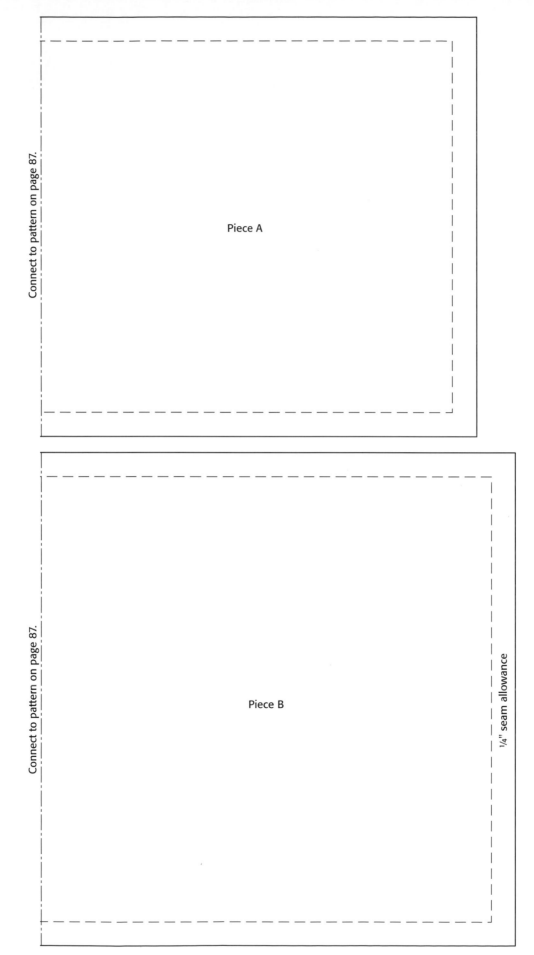

Connect to pattern on page 87.

Piece A

Connect to pattern on page 87.

Piece B

¼" seam allowance

Dot to Dot

"Dots" come in all forms, from shiny wet pebbles on the beach to the red polka-dot dress you had in first grade. Buttons can be dots as well, and who doesn't have a collection of buttons? Here we used dichroic glass buttons as tactile dots, connected by colorful silk ribbons. They add sparkle and mischievous pleasure, reminding me of those dot-to-dot puzzles we all did as kids.

—Joan

Pieced by Joan Segna. Quilted by Sandy Sims.

Finished quilt: 41½" x 62½"

Materials

Yardage is based on 42"-wide fabric.

- ⅞ yard of dark fabric for border

- 12 coordinating fat quarters for blocks

- 2¾ yards of fabric for backing

- ⅝ yard of fabric for binding

- 48" x 69" piece of batting

- 15 pieces of ½"- to ¾"-wide silk ribbon, 1¾ yards long

- 35 buttons (See "Resources" on page 95 for information on dichroic glass buttons.)

- 27 yards of ¼"-wide lightweight fusible-web tape

Cutting

All measurements include ¼" seam allowances. Refer to the block placement guide on page at right as you cut. Press the 12 fat quarters and layer them one on top of another so that no two similar colors are layered next to each other. You will cut two layers at once, beginning with the top two fat quarters from the stack. Place each block on a design wall after cutting, following the block placement guide. It's a good idea to number each block as you cut. Mark either on the fabric in the seam allowance, on a piece of tape stuck to each piece, or on a slip of paper pinned to each piece.

From the top 2 fat quarters, cut:

2 rectangles, 5½" x 8½" (blocks 1 and 4)

2 rectangles, 5½" x 13½" (blocks 11 and 23)

From the next 2 fat quarters, cut:

2 squares, 8½" x 8½" (blocks 2 and 3)

2 rectangles, 5½" x 8½" (blocks 12 and 14)

2 rectangles, 8½" x 13½" (blocks 22 and 25)

From the next 2 fat quarters, cut:

2 squares, 8½" x 8½" (blocks 5 and 18)

1 square, 5½" x 5½" (block 13)

1 rectangle, 5½" x 13½" (block 24)

From the next 2 fat quarters, cut:

2 rectangles, 8½" x 13½" (blocks 6 and 7)

2 rectangles, 5½" x 8½" (blocks 15 and 17)

2 squares, 8½" x 8½" (blocks 26 and 28)

From the next 2 fat quarters, cut:

2 rectangles, 8½" x 13½" (blocks 8 and 16)

1 rectangle, 3½" x 8½" (block 19)

1 rectangle, 5½" x 8½" (block 27)

From the last 2 fat quarters, cut:

2 rectangles, 5½" x 13½" (blocks 9 and 10)

2 rectangles, 8½" x 13½" (blocks 20 and 21)

From the border fabric, cut:

3 strips, 5½" x 42"

3 strips, 2½" x 42"

From the binding fabric cut:

6 strips, 2¼" x 42"

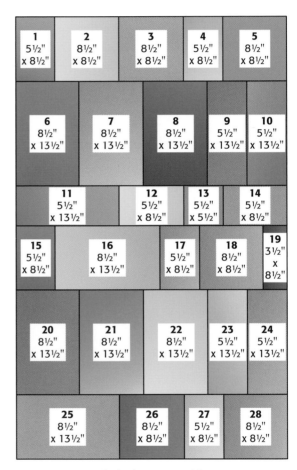

Block placement guide

Assembling the Quilt

1. Study the blocks on the design wall and adjust the color balance, if necessary, by swapping like-sized squares or rectangles. You can also cut new blocks from scraps if desired.

2. Sew the blocks into rows, pressing the seams to one side. Sew the rows together. Press the seams in one direction.

3. To mark a grid for the ribbon, begin at the bottom left-hand corner and measure up the left side of the quilt. Referring to ribbon diagram 1 for the next steps, add placement marks at 13", 18", 31", and 44".

4. From the bottom left-hand corner, measure across the bottom and place marks at 13", 18", and 31".

5. From the top left-hand corner, measure across the top and place marks at 3", 8", 21", and 26".

6. From the bottom right-hand corner, measure up the right side and place marks at 9½", 24", 29", 42", and 47".

7. Use a ruler and chalk to draw lines connecting your placement marks.

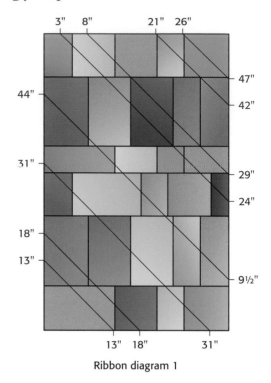

Ribbon diagram 1

8. Center the fusible tape, paper side up, along the chalk lines. Fuse in place with an iron, starting and stopping the fusible tape ½" from each edge.

9. Measure the lengths of the diagonal chalk lines. For the topmost line at upper right, cut one ribbon 9" longer than the measurement. For the 3 lines that extend across the lower left-hand corner, cut three ribbons 9" longer than the measurements. Cut the other four ribbons 1" longer than the line measurements. All but two ribbons will extend across a border.

10. Remove the paper from the fusible tape. Iron the ribbons to the fusible web, leaving border tails free at each end.

11. Refer to ribbon diagram 2 below to make placement marks for the ribbons running perpendicular to the ribbons just applied. Begin at the bottom right-hand corner to measure up the right side and make placement marks at 8", 21", 26", 39", and 52".

12. From the bottom right-hand corner, measure to the left along the bottom and make placement marks at 8", 21", and 26".

13. From the top left-hand corner, measure across the top and make placement marks at 10" and 23".

14. From the top left-hand corner, measure down the left side and make placement marks at 10", 23", 38", and 51".

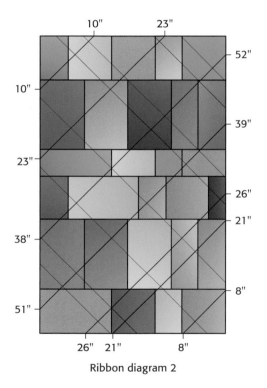

Ribbon diagram 2

15. Use a ruler and chalk to draw lines connecting your placement marks.

16. Center the fusible tape, paper side up, over the chalk lines. Fuse in place with an iron, starting and stopping the fusible tape ½" from each edge.

17. Measure the lengths of the diagonal chalk lines. Cut the two ribbons for the upper left-hand corner to the length measured plus 1". Cut the next two ribbons that extend across one border 9" longer than the measured length. Cut the three ribbons that extend across both borders in the lower right-hand corner 16" longer than the measured length.

18. Remove the paper from the fusible-web tape. Place the ribbon on the fusible web and iron it in place, leaving ½" free at each end so that the ribbon isn't fused into the seam allowance.

19. Pin the "tail" back on the ribbons that extend into the right-hand and bottom borders so that they won't be caught in the seam when sewing the borders.

20. Measure the quilt top for borders as instructed in "Adding Borders" on page 16. Piece and cut one 5½" side-border strip to the required length and stitch it to the right-hand side of the quilt top. Piece and cut one 2½" side-border strip to the required length and stitch it to the left-hand side of the quilt top. Press toward the borders.

21. Cut one 2½" border strip for the top border to the required length and stitch it to the top edge of the quilt top. Cut one 5½" border strip for the bottom border to the required length and stitch it to the bottom edge of the quilt top. Press toward the borders.

22. With ruler and chalk, mark the ribbon lines that extend across the right-hand and bottom borders.

23. Cut appropriate lengths of ¼" fusible-web tape, center them over the chalk lines, and fuse in place, stopping ½" from the edge of the quilt.

24. Remove the paper from the web and fuse the ribbon extensions in place.

Finishing

Refer to "Finishing Your Quilt" on pages 19–21 for details as needed.

1. Prepare the backing, piecing it with a horizontal seam. Layer and baste the quilt with the batting and backing.

2. Hand or machine quilt in your favorite style. Follow the ribbon placement as part of the quilting scheme. You can quilt ribbons down the center, quilt them at each edge, or quilt over them as part of an overall quilting pattern.

3. Make and attach the binding.

4. Embellish the quilt with buttons at each ribbon intersection, including the ribbon intersection in the wide borders, referring to the quilt diagram at right and the photograph on page 89 for placement.

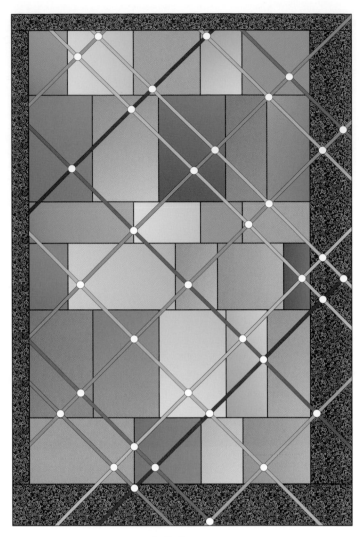

Quilt diagram

Resources

BELLA NONNA PETALS

Bella Nonna Design Studio
608 S. Jefferson
Kennewick, WA 99336
509-374-4369
www.bellanonnaquilt.com

FABRICS, FABRIC PAINTS, and DYES

Dharma Trading Company
P.O. Box 150916
San Rafael, CA 94915
800-542-5227
www.dharmatrading.com

POLKA-DOT RIBBONS

Renaissance Ribbons
www.renaissanceribbons.com

M&J Trimming
www.mjtrim.com

HAND-DYED RIBBONS

Artemis Exquisite Embellishments
5155 Myrtle Ave.
Eureka, CA 95503
888-233-5187
www.artemisinc.com

DICHROIC GLASS BUTTONS

Geddes Studio
9472 Golden Dr.
Orangevale, CA 95662
916-988-3355
www.geddesstudio.com

BEADS

Aspen Hot Glass Studio
www.aspenhotglass.com

SILK FABRIC

Hands of the Hills
3016 78 Ave. SE
Mercer Island, WA 98040
206-232-8121
www.handsofthehills.com

Meet the Authors

Joan Segna, left, and Jayme Crow, right, met in 1994 while working for Pacific Northwest National Laboratory in Richland, Washington. It didn't take long for them to discover a mutual love of fabrics, sewing, and design, and they often talked about collaborating their creative efforts. In the fall of 1999, they launched their business, Bella Nonna Design Studio. They began with "Purely for Pleasure" workshops at a bed-and-breakfast, using the parlor as their classroom. Students were treated to tea, homemade scones, and a masseuse, along with personalized quilting lessons. At their third workshop, they introduced their first Bella Nonna pattern and were on their way to creating a line of quilt patterns.

In 2001, Joan and Jayme displayed their new line of quilt patterns at International Quilt Market. Since then, they have enjoyed expanding their niche in the quilting world. *Stitch and Split Appliqué* is their first book, and this is their second.

Acknowledgments

We would like to thank the following people:
  Sandy Sims, our machine quilter extraordinaire
  Jerrine Kirsch, our "quilting tips and tricks" expert
  Our "studio helpers," Fallon Berglin, Kristin Berglin, Rachel Berglin, Lindsay Cook, Lexi Montgomery, Megan Cook, Hannah Leonard, Heidi Leonard, Leeann Linse, Alex Livingston, Sierra Montgomery, and Shannon Reilly. Thank you for your creative ideas and enthusiastic help!
  A very special friend and helper, Janette Gainey—you've made a wonderful contribution to our success.
  Our husbands, Don Segna and Jim Crow. You faithfully help and support us behind the scenes and take us out to dinner when we have quilted too long to cook.
  The Martingale family, with their expertise and enthusiastic support.

Our thanks to the following for graciously sharing products with us:
  Alexander Henry Fabrics; Andover Fabrics; Benartex, Inc.; Blank Textiles; Artemis Exquisite Embellishments; Bold Over Batiks!; Clearwater Fabrics; Diamond Textiles; Fabric Vision; Fabri-Quilt, Inc.; Firefly LLC; Geddes Studio; Gütermann of America, Inc.; Incomparable, Inc.; Island Batiks; Marcus Brothers Textiles, Inc.; Maywood Studio; Northcott Silk, Inc.; Red Rooster; Robert Kaufman; Sulky of America; Superior Threads, Textile Creations, Inc.; Tsukineko, Inc.; the Warm Company; and YLI Corporation.